The Different Levels of Death and Suicide

Wendy Terry

Happy Publishing

THE DIFFERENT LEVELS OF DEATH AND SUICIDE

ISBN: 978-0-9996603-5-5

Cover design by Deryn Bothe

Interior Design by Noel Morado

Names in this book have been changed from the original. The stories are based on experiences of the author.

Published by Happy Publishing
www.HappyPublishing.net

Dedication

I would like to dedicate this book to all my loved ones who have passed before me, especially my dear sweet grandparents who work with me every day.

To Mike, Mrs. Libby, Thora, Kyle, Nick and Charlie special spirits who work with me often and have shown me so much.

To every spirit that has ever connected with me and the people to whom I have given messages.

To my clients who have allowed me to be their medium, allowing themselves to receive the messages.

To everyone who gave me permission to use their experiences in this book.

To the one who gave me the gift of sight, so I could "see beyond".

Special thanks to my loved ones on earth for believing in me and allowing me to be myself.

To everyone who has supported me in any way.

To Dianne – I will always be grateful for you for asking me to work in your shop and for helping me on my professional journey.

To Sue – thank you for starting out with me on my tarot card reading and meditation journey.

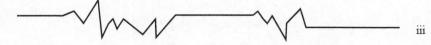

To Jeneen – thank you for always pushing me to go further and beyond what I thought was possible.

To Meaghan – thank you for being an incredible student and for helping me at many of my shows and meditation classes.

To my wonderful family immediate and extended, thank you for all the love and good times!

To my cousin and sister Sandra – Thank you for all your support and love always; no matter how far or near we are.

To my parents Brian and Deanna, thank you for all your love; for being there for me and not shutting me down, even if you did not understand. Thank you Mum for being supportive and for coming to many of my shows, thank you for our endless chats.

To my brothers Mike and Chris –I love you very much - thank you for being there for me when I was scared and for closing the curtains! I am grateful for you both.

To Kym – thank you for being the father of my daughters and for being a big part of my life.

To my beautiful daughters, Mandy, Melissa and Catherina – I love you beyond worlds. Thank you for coming along with me to some of my events and for all your help; to Catherina for finding the courage to give some of your own messages; to each one of you for guiding me to your friends so I could help and give them messages. I am so proud of you all for being such caring beings and doing this journey with me.

To Steve – thank you for taking me deeper so I can fly higher!

To you, for having an open mind and for making a difference; thank you for reading this book.

Acknowledgements

Thank you to Jillian Harris and Carol Chapman for reading over some of the chapters in this book and for your input in helping me with the editing. I am so happy to have you both in my life.

Thank you to Deryn Bothe for your graphic design work; I appreciate you bringing my vision into reality on the first try! Now that is truly one great designer!

Thank you to Hayley Porteous of Flair Photography for your very generous offer to take my picture for this book. I am grateful for you and the beautiful person you are.

Thank you to Erica Glessing of Happy Publishing for publishing this book. You definitely went above and beyond and made it very easy for me as a first time sole author (and someone who does not always comprehend technology) to get this book out into the world. You are simply amazing!

To you all – There are no words to say how much you fill my heart with joy; you are all such a special part of this book.

Table of Contents

Table of Contents

Table of Contents

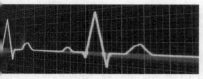

My life as a medium began when I was a very young girl although I did not know what it was called at the time. I was born in England to my wonderful parents Brian and Deanna who were so full of love. I am lucky as my life has always been surrounded by love.

From the time I could remember I could see people, people who I could see through! This would scare me and I would call for my Mum but she could not see them and reassured me that no one was there.

My two brothers Mike and Chris got to share a bedroom together. I remember always thinking that I wanted a sister but only because I wanted to share a room with someone too so that I did not have to be alone; alone with those faces when I went to sleep.

I was not born into a family of psychics so this was unfamiliar territory for everyone.

As I got older I would say to my friends "can you see that?" and they would say no so slowly I knew to keep things to myself. The night time scared me as I could see the faces even more; nothing was distracting me like the daytime – in the daytime we keep busy we have noise and other people to distract us. We moved to a lovely house which my Dad built when I was twelve. I had a big bedroom with a large window and sometimes when my parents had friends over and we had been allowed to stay up late I would get my brothers to go into my bedroom and close the curtains for me so I could not see the faces outside my window looking in.

We lived next door to an elderly couple called Mr and Mrs Libby. They were just lovely. I would go visit with them and Mrs. Libby told me that she read tea leaves. One day she visited my parent's house when we had family over and she read their tea leaves. She told my Auntie that she could see her in hospital and not to worry because she was going to be ok. My Auntie's jaw dropped because no one knew she was to go into hospital for an operation. I became fascinated by Mrs Libby; how could she see all that from a bunch of tea leaves? It was not until years later that I realized that Mrs Libby opened up another world to me; a world of seeing beyond!

My family moved to Canada when I was fifteen and a few years later my Mum had a card reading party. I was so fascinated by this and loved it all.

When I was eighteen my Grandfather who lived in England passed away; even though I was in Canada at the time I knew that he had died – somehow from somewhere deep inside of me I knew he had left this earth. He had not been sick so his death was unexpected. His death really affected me and I sobbed how could he have left us? Immediately that night I felt his presence with me, this scared me as I felt he was coming to get me. I jumped up out of the darkness of the night and screamed for my Mum making the excuse I was sick with a pain in my stomach. She said "Wendy what is really going on?" I told her Granfer (the name I called my Grandfather) was in my room and I was scared. My Mum told me that even if that were true (as she could not see what I could) he would never hurt me as he loved me. That made sense to me and I eased back to my room. Neither of us understood what was really happening as we had no knowledge of this type of thing and did not know anyone else who could see spirit. From that night on I could never be alone in a house, in the dark, by myself. I would stay awake until I knew someone else was home.

A few years later when I was married my husband would frequently go away to work and I would be left alone. I had to go to bed with a night light on as well as the TV and then maybe I would fall asleep about three in the morning. After I had my first child I was ok because now there was another human presence in the house and I had someone to get up with, to nurse and look after. A year later we moved to a bigger house in the country and the fear started all over again, it was too quiet, I could hear voices and sounds. In our previous little house I could open the window and the traffic noise would distract me so I felt a false sense of security. It was not until years later when my third child was having her first sleep over at her friend's house (my other two daughters had gone away for the weekend) that I would be completely alone in the house again. I told my friend Jeneen that I probably would be awake all night. I did not want to say no to my youngest daughter just so I would not be alone. Jeneen said she would do Emotional Freedom Technique (EFT – a form of tapping with fingers on the end points of energy meridians) on me to take away my fear. So after a few rounds of tapping she cleared my fear of the dark. That night I slept in the house alone. I had left a light on but even had to turn that off! To this day I am still ok, the spirits don't scare me anymore as I have a better understanding of them.

I occasionally would still go to readers and still loved it.

After I had my third child my friend Sue asked if I wanted to learn how to read the tarot cards. I said sure I was on maternity leave after all. When I started to learn to read them the spirits started to come in stronger again and I would try to push them away, but they came stronger.

We went to a meditation class where it opened up another world to me. In that meditation loved ones who had passed over came through to us, I had thought my grandparents would be there and I was right but there was also a family friend I called my second Dad his name was Mike, he came to hug me and then my grandmother on my Dads side who had passed away when I was three came. (We did not really talk about her a great deal as a family as it was so long ago that she had passed away and therefore she did not really come into conversation – or at least not when I was around). All I know is she came to give me a hug and it was the most amazing loving hug I have ever felt. It was the hug I did not remember from her. She told me that she loved me very much and that she left early so I could became closer to my other grandmother so I would not feel guilty over loving and spending more time with one than the other. I did become extremely close to my Gran; I felt I loved her more than anyone and I got to spend many wonderful weekends with her. There were lessons for my Grandfather, Dad and Uncle to learn; some were learnt and some had not yet been learnt but she loved us all each and every one of us. My Grannie Harris told me her sign to me was a purple violet and when I saw this she would be around. It shocked me that I had seen her as I was not expecting that at all. When I came out of the meditation I cried, well actually I did not cry, I sobbed.

I remember stopping at my parent's house late at night on my way home because I could not believe that I had seen my grandmother and wanted to tell my Dad; I was so excited. My Dad listened intently and wanted to know what else she had said. So even thought my parents did not always get this they never told me they did not believe and always allowed me to talk.

As my journey continued and I started working with the tarot cards; one day I said "ok spirits I am now really ready to let you in". Well what continued after that was a series of scary events for me. The spirits came in all right; I thought they were going to kill me.

As I lay in sleep half-awake half asleep a male would come and try and suffocate me, placing his hand over my mouth. I would try and scream with all my might and finally fling myself out of bed. This got worse and I thought if this is what this type of stuff is bringing to me then I am quitting. One evening I had a sumo wrestler try-ing to attack me. I remember biting his finger and all I could taste was the salt from his sweat! I did not pick the cards up again for six weeks. Then somewhere inside of me I heard a voice say "but Wendy this is who you are, this is part of your life purpose."

I told one of my co-workers at the bank where I worked about my experience. She was a member of the Catholic Church and she gave me some holy water to put beside my bed. Then I heard "you are stronger than they are and you have free will put a white light of protection up around yourself." So I continued with the cards and connecting again; I would imagine myself in a bubble of protective white light. One night my daughter was having a sleep over at our house with some of her friends (my husband was out of town with work). I set up beds downstairs for us all to sleep. When the young ones were asleep and I began to fall asleep I became aware of a male spirit coming towards me with a pillow to try and suffocate me. He put the pillow over my face but I had been lying on my side and had an air hole through which I could breathe I remembered about the white light of protection and put that around me he started to take a step backward away from me and continued until he was gone. To this day I have never had that problem again.

I continued to do readings for family and friends until one day my neighbour Dianne opened up a spa shop. She asked me if I would come and do some readings in her shop. At first I said no, how could I charge for my readings? But she encouraged me and finally I said yes. From day one I had clients and through word of mouth my clientele grew until I had a huge waiting list. From there life continued to change. I studied how to do meditation classes and then taught them myself, loving every minute of it; taking people on a spiritual journey while giving them messages at the same time. This gave me great fulfilment.

I went on a course with James Van Praagh, a famous medium in California. It was an amazing class and for me it gave me the confidence to see that I could also do what he did. In one meditation Merlin channelled through me and it was as though I was looking out of his eyes, they were very blue and he had lots of wrinkles around his eyes. I was amazed as to why he would channel all that wisdom and knowledge to me – why me? Now years later I think why not me!

One day I found out that someone I knew whose husband was sick and hospitalized, was having financial difficulties. So I thought how can we help this family? My best friend and business partner Jeneen Yungwirth has also been doing this journey with me (her book on Amazon is called "You are not alone") decided we could do a message show and all the proceeds would go to this family. Well this was the first time we were on stage and was I nervous. Jeneen had gone to the bathroom and I was all alone in the theatre before the show started and I thought I can't do this! In my head I shouted if I am meant to do this then you have to give me a sign! All of a sudden I heard a voice say turn around. When I did there was a chalk board off to the side and the name Harris was written on that board (the surname of my Grandmother). Also beside it was a pair of glasses (like the ones my other grandmother used to wear) and a daisy (my grandmother on my Mum's side her sign to me) I trusted them and knew it would be ok. We did the show and had amazing results, making the family a few thousand dollars. This would prove to be the first of many shows we would do, sometimes together and sometimes doing our own shows.

Now my life has bought me back to England where I was again guided by spirit. This has given me the opportunities to go back and forth between Canada and England working with clients while gathering and learning more about the different levels of spirit enabling me to write this book to share with you.

I believe everything happens for a reason although it is hard to see what that reason could be when you are going through some of life's rough experiences.

My learning continues; I now do energy therapies with people teaching how to release emotional blockages they carry from past lives, ancestors and this life time. I love helping people so they can live happier, peaceful, more fulfilling lives.

May you enjoy these true life stories of just a few of the experiences that I have witnessed. (Some names have been changed for privacy issues; Mum and Mom are spelt how the story requires it to be). May it open you up to a whole new world of beyond – opening your mind to a new perspective that maybe; just maybe there is more to life than we think!

With much love to you all, Wendy xo

Chapter 1
A Privilege or A Hurt?

To understand whether it is a privilege or a hurt you must have a deep spiritual connection with someone.

To me my grandparents on my mother's side were so very special to me. I would spend weekends with them; my grandfather would spend hour's playing cards and dominoes with me. My Gran would teach me how to crochet and knit. My Gran would take me to Sunday school along with my brothers. I remember my brothers saying they did not want to go anymore. They were more interested in football, but I still wanted to go. It excited me even more to think I got to spend a Saturday night with my grandparents all by myself. I loved it. I felt spoilt with love and their affection. I could have these memories all for myself. One day as a teenager I remember telling my Gran I did not want to go to Sunday school any more either but still wanted to sleep over, I was nervous as I knew she loved going to church and singing, would she still love me? Would she be mad? When I told her she understood, happy I still wanted to come and spend the night, even though we lived in the same town.

I remember going to spend Saturday nights, staying up late at their house, eating my favourite things – crisps! (Potato chips) My Gran used to buy three different flavours not knowing which my favourite was, I never told her because I used to eat them all! I used to love our bedtime ritual where they had three easy chairs in front of the warm open fire, my Gran and I had beef Oxo and Granfer had buttery sops. When Gran got home from Church we would have a roast meal and me and Gran had rice pudding for dessert and Granfer Semolina. This may have seemed simple but it bonded us together on a deeper level.

I remember one day when I was in the living room watching TV with them there was a picture of my parents on their wedding day on the wall. I would say" look can you see that?" I could see the reflection of the ceiling light in the photo and it would swing very fast from side to side; "can you see it?" I would even get them to change seats with me so that they could see it, but they could not. I was never scared by this just fascinated how could I see it but they could not?

I loved them both so very much, with everything I had in me. Maybe because I knew they loved me so deeply. They were wonderful. Sometimes people have favourites but I knew they loved all their grandchildren the same; a different bond with each one; inside me I knew I was very connected to them, now I understand in a spiritual way.

When my family moved to Canada our taxi picked us up from their place and somehow me and Gran found ourselves alone in her bedroom (this still brings me to tears now as I write this) and I remember my Gran just hugged me and cried. To you this might not mean much but to me at fifteen this was the first time I had ever seen my Gran cry. She was a tough women and I think I am still the only one who has ever saw her cry; so the question is, is this a privilege or a hurt? I carry her in my heart as I do everyone and I feel blessed that she would show me her vulnerability and trust me, knowing I loved her and would never judge her. Feeling grateful that she would show me how much she would miss me.

As I said in the introduction I knew when my Grandfather died I felt it on some level. I was so thankful that my Mum told me that he would not hurt me. That made sense to me and after that I let him visit me. Luckily he still visits me to this day.

My Gran and Granfer had been married for fifty years, yes they bickered but oh how they loved each other, after my Grandfather died my Gran came to Canada and stayed with us for three months. I had been engaged so she got to meet my fiancé at the time. When she returned to England she was not herself. She missed my Grandfather and started to decline. I was getting married in the May, I hoped she could hang on, but much to my dismay she passed away in the December. I was angry why she got to see my cousin who was not as close to her in Canada get married and not me! I knew we were connected spiritually, so why? Well she came to see me. I felt her hand over hand feeling the edge of my bed one day as I was falling asleep. It made my heart beat fast – was it fear or excitement that she was there. Later in life as I understood more, I understood her sign to me were daisies. When I looked back on my wedding day the bridesmaids flowers were made of daisies. She was there all along.

I was angry when she died, how dare she leave me! I missed her! Today with the knowledge that I have I would have been happy for her, knowing that she was reunited with her husband whom she loved so much.

So yes they really are always a blessing! Thank you for loving me, thank you for loving me even deeper after death, in ways I did not see at the time.

As much as it can hurt at the time of their passing it is indeed a privilege to have loved so deeply.

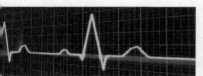

Chapter 2
The Many Ways of Spirit

The energy of spirit is simply amazing! There are endless ways that they try to come through.

Some of them will come through to their loved ones in dreams and sometimes when people are blocked with their emotions, spirit will come to other people who are open so they can pass a message on to their loved ones here on earth. So if you ever have a dream of a deceased person please pass the message on. When you have a dream of a loved one who has passed over they are having a visit with you; if they pass a message to you I would pay full attention to what they are saying as they have now seen and know things on a higher level.

Messages take on different forms; sometimes you can smell spirit. Rachel's Dad would always come through in the smell of smoke because he always smoked a pipe. One evening Sam swore he could smell smoke while he was sleeping in his bedroom of his apartment. It was so strong that he got out of bed and went out into the hall way but there was no one there and no smoke smell out there either. Sam returned to the bedroom to the strong smell of the smoke again. It was not until the morning that he figured out it was his grandfather who he had never met and had smoked over a pack of cigarettes a day. Now Sam knows when that smoke smell occurs it is his grandfather coming around him and helping him with a situation in his life.

Helens Mum comes around in perfume; her favourite was lily of the valley, so whenever she smells that she knows her Mum is close by and it brings comfort to her. For Sonja her Grandmother comes through with the smell of freshly baked bread; this always takes Sonja back to her Grandmother's house when she was a little girl and brings the feeling of contentment to her.

Spirit will call your name. I am sure there are many of you who have sworn you have heard someone calling your name but no one is there. The phone can ring and the line can be static, most often it is spirit trying to communicate with you. Once I had a message left on my answering machine; the message was very static but you could hear a distinct male's voice saying "hellooooooooo". On one occasion I taped a reading for a client and I was telling her what she should have for breakfast. When she went home and played the tape she was astonished. She bought the tape back for me to listen to and in the pause of our conversation you could hear a man's voice saying what she should have for breakfast and then I said it!

Spirits can also do things electronically like turning up the TV, even changing the channel. They can flicker the lights and make noises around the house. Many can play with toys so they make sounds. My daughter used to have a Barney dinosaur toy that used to speak. Every once in a while for no apparent reason it would just speak. I would go into her room and it would just be sitting on her bed looking at me, it was like it was telling me to have more fun!

Many spirits will play songs on the radio; they talk to you through words. When you turn on the radio listen to the words, sometimes you will think of a deceased person (they put their name into your head because they are with you) it is them speaking to you so pay attention to what they want to say to you. Spirit can play their favourite songs around you to let you know they are right there with you. You might hear the song you chose for their funeral; it is their way of saying "thank you I liked the song you chose for me".

Spirits give you symbolic messages and many signs like flowers, animals, feathers, rainbows, bubbles, coins, numbers, cards, cars, balloons, colours and so much more.

At one of my shows a Mum came through and told her daughter her sign to her was the number 3. Three was very significant. I told the daughter Jo that the number three was a very high vibration number for her Mum and March was a very significant month. Jo confirmed her Mum liked the number three and she herself was meant to be born on March third. Jo's son had been born on March third. Jo now knows that when she sees the number 3 her Mum is around her.

Some spirits give the same sign to all their loved ones and some give a different sign to every family member. When my Uncle died he gave his wife and daughter the sign of a beautiful pink rose to remind them how much he loved them. To his son an owl for all the wisdom and the fact his son would be the head of the house now and all would look to him for his wisdom. To his grandsons he would give robins, for them to plant the seeds to their future and carry on his name and roots. To his daughter in law he gave a sun flower, for all the light she bought to their family and all the help she gives to his wife. If you do not know what your sign is you can ask for spirit to show you one and to bring it to your awareness. If not, you can ask them to show you something specific when they are around.

Some spirits are really cheeky and will hide things on you like your keys (I often find this is because you are in a hurry and stressed and it is their way of saying, slow down, catch your breath as everything will be fine). If you have lost something you can always ask them to show you where it is. You have to be still and quiet so the thought will come to your mind. They can move pictures to get your attention. They can even knock things out of your hands. At one of my message shows I had told Tracy that her Nan was throwing balls of wool at her, she said "yes it happened this morning when I went into my shop there were balls of wool lying all over the floor!"

Some spirits show themselves to you. This is the hardest of all as many block this because in their subconscious mind they are scared. You can always ask them to show themselves to you in your third eye so it is not as scary for you or to come in your dreams.

However they want to be known to you just allow it to flow. Appreciate the gifts and messages that spirit brings.

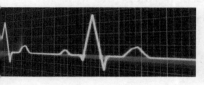

Chapter 3

Grief

There are many levels of grief and everyone grieves differently. Grief can make you sad and angry; you can grieve the loss of a job, a relationship, the loss of an animal, change in any way, as well as losing a loved one.

Everyone grieves differently so do it YOUR WAY! As time goes on you might be able to cope with the change and you can find things easier. You can have days where it is extremely difficult to cope with anything – on those days just be and allow yourself to go through the emotions. Maybe you just need a day to do nothing to sit and remember those treasured memories. Sit on the couch and feel your loved ones with you, bring them to you, have a day of being with them.

Many people suffer in silence not wanting to tell others about their feelings; for fear of being rejected. If you are one of these people find someone to talk to, even a stranger, about what is bothering you or the loved ones you are missing, it will make you feel better knowing that someone cares. If you are that person who listens and allows people to be themselves THANK YOU as you are making a huge difference.

Are you treating people the way you want them to treat you? If you want people to accept you are you accepting them the way they are? Remember everyone is different so no two people on this earth would do the exact same thing. You don't have to agree with them but it is important not to resist them, their ideas and opinions just allow people to be and have them.

If ten people watched the same movie and had to write down their experience all ten would be different they would have seen and heard and remembered different things about the movie.

Receive you and allow yourself to be you and grieve in your own way; treat yourself with kindness; nothing is right or wrong it just is.

When someone that we love so much leaves the physical world it becomes very strange to us because a part of us left – our energy has changed and it can never go back to the way it was. When someone is etched into our soul we have to learn to go on with an emptiness inside, missing them, aching for them. Trying to be strong for others while feeling we are falling apart on the inside.

As time goes on you can have "good days" and there will be days when you miss them so much you want to scream – "can anyone understand?" I know many people who still grieve after years of their loved ones dying and the hardest thing for them is when people say to them "you should be over it already". So just allow yourself to grieve at your own pace and at your own level.

We have all lost people. Some are just etched on the surface so it will be easier to get over but for the ones etched on the soul level it will never be the same again until you meet on the other side or in a future life time.

My Auntie lost her husband someone she worked and loved with every day. When he died you could literally see that a part of her had died too. She copes with life and does day to day things but inside her eyes, inside her soul she yearns to be with him. She will feel complete and happy and her soul alive when her soul and his soul connect again.

For people who can meditate and connect to the other side it can be much easier. For myself I can sit here and bring my loved ones to me. Do I have days that I miss them? Yes I do even years after their death. I tell them I love and miss them and bring them close to me. I close my eyes and feel their love, I smell them as if they are here on earth and I can see them. I ask them questions and allow the answers to come at their own pace, sometimes it can be days later but I just go with it. I pay attention to how the answers show up in my life. The more you do this the easier it will become for you do what works for you; if you have a Dad who used to fix cars go into the meditation with him fixing a car and see yourself hanging around talking to him; I like to have a cup of tea with my Gran as that is what we often did in this life time. This is a place where you can feel their love; if you are missing their hugs go in and hug them and feel the love inside of you.

Just be you and grieve in your own space and time, do not be ashamed of how you feel, after all you were blessed on earth to have loved that deeply! So carry the treasures and love with you as they will always be in your heart for you to get at any time you wish and NO ONE can take that away from you.

Chapter 4
Healing for Peace

L ois first met me when she came to me for a reading; her husband had come through for her saying he was sorry for everything that had happened. I told Lois it was time for her to let go, it was time for her to heal. On the outside Lois was a very gentle woman but underneath she was angry; something she did not want to show the outside world. Many people want to be happy and gentle; they don't like to be angry but the truth is people do get angry and upset and it is to learn how to release this emotion. I told Lois it was ok to scream. The next day Lois called to say that on the way home in her car she really did scream; even when she got home and was having a bath this screeching scream came out of her voice; so much so that the light bulb blew! She had no idea the extent of this emotion that she had been carrying.

Lois had told me that she had lung cancer and heard I was starting doing Reiki and other healing modalities; she asked if I could help her in that respect also. I asked two other friends who practised healing energy work if they would help me with Lois; which they were happy to do. When Lois' husband passed away she found out he had an affair on her. The first energy session was intense where we helped Lois clear a lot of anger toward her husband for the deceitful things he had done to her and the shame he had bought to her family. Lois wanted to be perfect; she did not want the world to see otherwise. I was new to Reiki; it was moving energy in people; you had to work with symbols. To me I followed what I was told to do in class but as soon as the class was over I worked my way. I allowed spirit to guide me with each client; listening to what needed to be released; what emotion they were carrying so we could work on healing that energy block. I could see black things being released and removed from people. I sometimes had no clue why I was working this way or why things would happen; all I knew I had to follow the energy for each client. Every single client was different.

I was convinced that we would help with Lois and her healing; we worked on Lois about four times and each time we cleared emotions and feelings within her that she had shoved down.

Shockingly to me Lois passed away! I was stunned, what? How can that be? Why did we work on her if we could not save her? What was the purpose of releasing her anger when she was going to die anyway? We had done some amazing energy work on Lois. The power of three was magnificent; we had all witnessed things we had never seen before, never experienced! It was indeed profound – so why? Why did she have to die?

A little while later one of Lois' daughters came to me for a reading; I did not know who she was but Lois came through. It was quite emotional for me because Lois told me that we did "save" her. Because of the healing energy work that we had performed she was able to let go and heal on a cellular level; she was able to die with no emotional baggage; she had an easy transition to the other side; a very peaceful one. For me I was very grateful for Lois as I had learnt so many things from her and her journey which was still continuing as she was now helping her daughters with their healing journey.

Over the years both Lois and her husband have come through many times for their daughters with significant pieces bringing peace.

Chapter 5
Afraid to Talk

I received an email from a friend of mine overseas who had lost her dog that was very close to her, Andrea admitted she was afraid to talk to her family as they were telling her to get over it already! To her the dog had been her baby, her child, he had a human personality! She connected to him at a soul level and she did not feel complete anymore now that he was gone. Andrea knew it sounded crazy but very much felt this dog had been her child in a past life. She had three dogs in total. Andrea loved them all but this one was special, this one was different – it was like they could communicate on a telepathic level. How could she explain that to anyone? Andrea was so afraid to talk. She was sad all the time. All Andrea could manage to do was go to work, come home and sleep. Her family were not letting her be herself and grieve in her own way. Andrea wanted to talk about her beloved dog but they had enough and would not listen. All they needed to do was let her talk! (Her family did not have to say anything). It helped Andrea to talk to me but in all honesty it only helped for a day or two as she needed to continue to talk and keep talking and talk some more.

Animals are souls, they all have different personalities. It is true they are like the human soul so when you have a deeper relationship with an animal you will grieve deeper.

Our friends recently lost their dog Ozzy. It was a terrible thing for them to go through as he had been "their child" together; he was "their baby". He loved to play ball even right up until he died. Unfortunately he had a huge cancerous growth that had erupted and became infected. Ozzy had to be put down. Mandy and Shaun made the choice to be with him, to hold him, so he could be peaceful as his mind was very much alive. The grief and sadness was almost unbearable for them. They were used to coming home every lunch hour to let their dog out and they no longer needed to do that, instead they would come home to an empty cold house. They saw reminders of Ozzy around the house, his balls, his food, but could not face getting rid of anything yet. This to them was worse than anything they had gone through. They were also aware that they could not speak to everyone about how sad they were because they would get the answer "but it is only a dog." I went to Mandy and Shaun's' house to see them, I wanted to see if Ozzy's spirit was there but he was not. The house was indeed cold and empty. A couple of evenings later, as I was writing for my book I felt Ozzy come into my awareness and he told me to say "I am coming home Dad!" I could see Ozzy healed and running towards his front door of the house. Then I channelled this poem from him.

> *Yes I was born to doggy parents*
> *But then I met my real parents*
> *They took me in and loved me unconditionally*
> *They bathed me and fed me*
> *They played ball with me*
> *And allowed me to sleep in their bed*
> *They gave me everything I needed*
> *One day I got sick*
> *They took me to the vet*

And loved me even more
They tried to save me and keep me here
But it was my time and I could not stay
I left something valuable behind
My paw print in their hearts
Forever bonded together
A treasure only we will remember

– I love you Mum and Dad, Ozzy

Ozzy had wanted me to frame this and put it with some of the photos I had taken of him a few days before he had passed, when Mandy and I had gone to the beach with him. A beach day that was unexpected. Mandy had phoned me to see if I wanted to go – I said I had a couple of hours in between clients so off we went. I told her we were making memories and I started to take pictures of Ozzy and her throwing the ball. This was the last time Ozzy would go to the beach. Somewhere there was a knowing.

A co-worker of mine had lost her son in a car accident and while we were talking about his death she said the hardest thing was when people would not say anything to her. I said when I was younger and people had died the truth was I did not know what to say. I did not want to upset people even more so I said nothing and just hugged them. Kathleen understood and said she was ok with that; it was when she started talking about her son that people would put their eyes to the floor and say nothing. She wanted to talk about him, she wanted to share stories about him; Kathleen wanted to keep parts of him alive. It kept her son close to her.

Death leaves a void that cannot be filled. No one can ever take the place of that person or animal in this world. We learn to adjust to the difference in our energy.

Chapter 6
I Believe in Angels

I believe in angels because I have always seen them. I work as one of their messengers, bringing messages to their loved ones here on earth. Some of you are skeptics and that is ok. I probably would have been if I had not had so many experiences connecting me to the other side; I have seen too much not to believe.

Every soul and spirit has a different purpose. When I was doing a group reading one evening a lady appeared in the corner of the room as soon as I entered. I asked the owner of the house if she had lost her Mum as I felt that was who was in the corner. She validated that she had passed and we started the readings with her Mum. The Mum then bought forward her brother who went to the niece and said one of the reasons he had passed was to be the protector and he gave me the vision of a dark blue four door car getting in a fender bender, spinning around and crashing , everyone was fine – it seemed they had been very lucky. The lady confirmed that this had happened; they had been lucky and had gotten out without a scratch! I told her he still gets in the car with her and she laughed saying she was a terrible driver! This was a validation that he was indeed protecting her on the roads.

For another person a grandfather came through to send a new born child to this earth. The child had a birth defect so no one understood how that could be; the grandfathers words were that he went before to save his grandchild and would be there with them in surgery. This grandchild did have to have a major operation in which he survived. The grandfather still watches over his family and makes sure everyone is ok.

One day while I was in Canada there was a major snow storm. From the window of my house this storm did not seem so bad; the snow was coming down heavy but I could still see a little of the road. I ventured out onto the highway as I had a full day of clients I did not want to let down. As I turned onto the highway the storm was indeed a lot worse than it looked from my window. The snow was blowing so much that it was a white out. I could not tell if I was on the road or close to the ditch, all I could see was white. I knew somehow I had to turn around and get back to my house; this was too dangerous to be out in. I had no idea if I had cars close to me or what side of the road I was on – all I knew is I was scared! I knew I had to get off the highway and get onto the side road which was close by somewhere. I had no idea how far away that side road was but I had to get to it. I shouted to my angels "please present a clearing to me so I can get onto the side road" I screamed for them to show it to me now. With that a peaceful clearing appeared and it was right where the side road was. As soon as this clearing appeared a sense of peace came over me. I was no longer scared, instead I was very calm. I slowly got onto the side road and made my way back to my house. I was so grateful to the angel who had appeared and presented the clearing to me.

Another time I was driving to work; I was eight months pregnant with my daughter Melissa when I hit some black ice and skidded across the road. All I can tell you was it was like my car was flying; flying high in the air in slow motion. I had the thoughts that I could die in this moment; what would my young daughter Mandy be like without me? Would the baby inside of me live or die? Then a beautiful light came over me, this gave me the most peaceful feeling that I have ever experienced. With that I landed on the other side of the road and my car bounced – it bounced right over the railway tracks! The car bounced a few more times and came to a standstill. I still remained peaceful, I got out of my car immediately and went to the road and started walking to work. A man from my community picked me up and offered to take me to the hospital. I was fine I just wanted to get to work. The man was concerned as he said the car should not have landed where it did and I was lucky there were no on coming vehicles. I was so lucky! The baby and I were good and I only had a tiny scratch on my finger from this accident. I was very grateful to the 'presence' who had guided my vehicle to safety!

Angels appear in all forms; they can look like angels, our loved ones, there are earth angels who walk among us here on earth. I know that each one is special and I appreciate all their love, kindness, peace and protection as they help us here on earth.

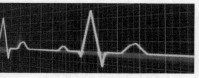

Chapter 7

Regrets

I have talked to many people who have lost loved ones and they have regretted something. If this is you take a moment and heal. You can write to your loved one who has passed on a letter about your feelings and then you can burn it and throw the ashes away outside as a release.

If you have someone on earth you are not talking to, then take a moment and ask yourself how would you feel if they died? Would you have any regrets? If so reach out to them, send them a card or call them. However, if they don't respond to you then it is their issue and you must have no regrets because that is what they are choosing.

Ask yourself if you died, as it can happen at any moment, would you be happy with your life? Would you be happy with the way you have treated people? Would you be happy with what you have done? Is there something you would like to do before you die? If so take an action step and do it! Prioritize what is really important to you.

I have had loved ones in spirit come through and apologize for their behaviours on Earth. Yes sometimes it is lessons to be learnt but other times it can be ego or stubbornness.

One husband came through to say he always had to be right no matter what. He created a life of misery, NEVER seeing his wife's point of view. He was the one that mattered, he had to be right! He never saw that he created misery for his wife. He never saw that she was the one that gave in all the time. He never saw how much she compromised. He never realized how much he loved her because he could not see through his own screen of fog he had created for himself. He was sorry and did love her even though he could have shown her more. If he had the chance to do it all over again he would have done it differently. So even though this husband had created some of the wife's pain, she could start her healing journey with her husband by her side.

It is so important to let go of regret and not dwell in it. We all learn from situations and I am sure we have all said at one time "I would never do that now" – well that is because you have learnt from it. You needed that piece to happen so you could be the person you are today. We can only do our best with the tools that we have. That is why it is always great to keep learning. I always say take the love and the lessons and leave everything else behind. Look forward not backwards. Looking to the past is good only when healing or holding on to happy loving memories. If you are going to make a difference in this world; enjoy living in the moment while planning how to be happier. Be happy right now! Regrets cannot survive in happy. If you don't know what makes you happy try doing new things; if you try something new and you don't like it then don't do it again; but keep trying; keep looking – never give up – because guaranteed you will find happy! There are many levels of happy; so continue going higher and higher. When you get to happy enjoy it while continuing your journey to happier – keep going. Often people say "this is the happiest I have ever been" and they stop at that level. I encourage you all to keep going; you will leave all your regrets behind.

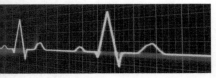

Chapter 8

Resentment

From doing my work I have learnt there are different places, levels and dimensions in the spirit world.

At one of my message evenings I received the message "Happy Birthday" so I asked the audience "whose birthday is it today?" A lady said it was her sister's birthday. I immediately had her Mother coming in from spirit saying tell your sister 'Happy Birthday' from me. Joan informed me her sister was on the other side as was her Mum. I told her they were not together and not in the same place. She said that it made sense as they were not talking to each other when they died. I very much felt forgiveness was needed for the sister, who had passed, so she could move to a higher level on the other side. Joan could not believe that would come up as she had that day told her sister she forgave her for the first time. I told her to continue to do it for a few days and even write her sister a letter and burn it in a green candle for healing. The sister had crossed over when she had died but she had gone to the first level on the other side as she was holding on to all this resentment towards her Mum. I see the first level as a heavier, darker level.

This is where souls go when they hold on and die with negative emotions inside of them such as anger, unforgiveness, resentment, greed, judgement, shame and blame. When Joan started to forgive her sister this not only set Joan's energy free on earth where she could be happier but it released her sister's energy into a higher level. When we set the spirit soul free they can then send greater blessings to us here on earth as they go higher into the light.

At one of my shows I had a mother come through for her daughter. The mother showed me that she had been very sick and the daughter had held her hand while she died. Two ladies had put their hands up to say this was their Mum. It is interesting how this can happen as they were sitting one in front of the other. This message was for both of them from each of their Mothers. I could see that there were other family members who had not been there for their Mum and these ladies were holding onto resentment for those family members. The Mum came through to say "let go, you were there for me. I know you did extra for me and I know how tired you were. I know how much you loved me. You have the memories and even though the other family members are mad at you now, they can never take those memories away from you. The other family members are upset because of the will and want the money. I know you don't want to fight so do not focus on their angry words and holding onto resentment because they were not there for me. They did not need to be. Instead hold onto the loving memories of me and you. Hold onto the fact I chose you to be there for me when I died because you really cared, you were strong enough to handle that, you were strong enough to see me take my last breath. The others could not have managed that last memory. It is ok, I love you all". Both these ladies understood this message it was as if their Mum took the resentment from their shoulders like removing a big weight and took it away. They both felt lighter, both had a sense of peace which they had not felt since their Mother's passing.

I had given a reading to Darlene and told her that her grandfather was with her holding a baby. She was not sure who the baby was but went home to ask her Auntie. It turned out this has been her Auntie's twin sister and it was her Auntie's Dad holding the baby. Darlene's Auntie had always blamed her Dad for her sister's death. The Auntie realized that her Dad had been holding onto this for all those years. She knew it was time to release him from those burdens. In the Aunties garden there were two identical trees one fully alive like her and one dead like her sister. The Auntie decided to forgive her Dad and put all her forgiveness and love into the dead tree. Months later Darlene came to show me a picture of the trees both now in full bloom and the one that was dead was now bigger and stronger than the other one. When we let go miracles can happen.

The lesson here is to not hold on to resentment. We must let go and forgive; we must forgive ourselves and others. In doing so we can be free and go higher when it is our time to go to another dimension.

Chapter 9
Unexpected Places

I had gone away for a weekend with Steve and our friends. We were celebrating mine and Amanda's March birthdays. We were having a fun relaxing time using the facilities spa and hot tub. In the evening we headed to the dining room for a fabulous supper. We were given a complimentary glass of champagne from the waiter and as he approached I let everyone know that the waiter had his Dad with him. This stuff always fascinated Amanda and Clive and they were very open to me talking about it. Sometimes I still resist giving people messages as I think this is my weekend off, but I also know that when I get this shaking inside of me that person needs to hear the message. As the waiter approached again I let him know that his Dad was with him and had a message for him. He acknowledged that his Dad had died a few months ago. I told him his Dad wanted him to know how very sorry he was as he had not accepted him and had been very wrong. He wanted to let him know he was with him and understood now. He was different and could see things differently from where he was. On Earth he just could not accept the fact that his son was different. He would help him now; he would help with easiness and acceptance. He was sorry he did not hug him when he was living and how he wished he could. He wanted him to let his Mum know that he was around her and sorry for the stress that he caused her because she accepted her son exactly how he was a lovely caring person! He was sorry for the stress that he had caused her in his sudden passing but he would be guiding her through the difficulties and all the paper work. The waiter left for about ten minutes and I was really hoping that I had not upset him too much as he had tears in his eyes and did not say anything else. He returned to the table to say "THANK YOU, you have no idea how that has helped me. My Dad did not accept me and we had a strained relationship which did indeed put stress on my Mum. I have just phoned my Mum to tell her and she is so happy to hear from him. My Dad did leave us suddenly and there is a mound of paperwork for my Mum to sort out." At the end of the evening we set up a Skype reading so I could continue to give messages to him, his Mum and sister from his Dad. I was very grateful to the waiters Dad for showing up in an unexpected place to help his son and for making such a huge difference in his life.

One year I was vacationing in Lanzarote with Steve and my parents. My Mum and I loved to do the morning aquacises in the pool, one morning while finishing these exercises we said hello to two ladies, Cat from Switzerland and her sister Ylan from Holland. I felt a very strong pull towards these ladies; while talking I could sense their grandmother with them and gave them messages from her. I gave Ylan messages to do with her daughter and the emotions she was enduring at the time – this made her cry as it was so true; I sat with them to teach them how to release their emotions. I told Ylan that we cannot control our children's journey – we have to let them go so they can grow. If we try to do everything for our children then we are saying we don't believe they can do it and are taking their power away. Yes would we love our children to have ease; absolutely but then maybe they would not learn the lesson they came to earth to do. We have all gone through something "hard" in this life time. If every single thing was easy then we would not learn from it. Ylan and Cat appreciated this very much and this helped them immensely. We became instant friends and are still connected. This was the first time I had given messages in a swimming pool! *I believe spirit helps us when needed.*

I have given many messages to people in public washrooms, pubs, shopping malls, spas, workplaces and restaurants to name a few.

On one occasion as I was waiting for my meal in a restaurant in Cornwall England (where they are very accommodating to dogs) I got this overwhelming sensation to look at the back of the room. I noticed this couple sat at a table with their Irish wolfhound dog. As a medium I never see the body I look past the body into the being. I could see the dog had the magical energy of Merlin and as his eyes met mine I felt him talk to my soul, my being. He was telling me to speak to his owners. This dog had wisdom so deep inside of him; he even had what looked like a long white beard! I introduced myself to his owners and told them what a magical dog they had; he had a being of deep wisdom and was more than 'just a dog'. They told me his name was Freddie. I said he had Merlin energy in him and his owners Rob and Sam agreed – they said sometimes it is like he is talking to us. I told Rob he could hear what Freddie was saying if he would just let go of his limitations. I told him his Dad was with him in spirit and he was saying he did not mean to give him limitations and it was time for him to step out of the family's beliefs. He still loved him but he was meant to be different from his limited family. Rob started to cry and thanked me. His Dad had died when he was twelve and the limitations were true. Sam said this is unbelievable as we just had this conversation today – I told Rob he could be more than he is and that he holds himself back. Rob and Sam were both amazed that this was both our first time in this pub and for us to be there at that precise moment together is how spirit works.

If you are aware you are carry limiting beliefs from your family, bless them, love them but give their limitations back to them knowing you can start to change your life from this moment forward — what can you do different? What would you like to bring into your life? Take actions steps to make this happen.

If spirit wants to get a message through to you they will find a way to orchestrate it. Be open to receiving at any given time!

Chapter 10
Messages in Dreams

While I was working at the bank, my co-workers Dad passed away. It was a very hard time for Debbie as she was so very close to him. Stanley had been in a wheelchair as he had multiple sclerosis and she would visit him and her Mom almost every day. Debbie had two daughters who were also very close to their Grandparents. Stanley was a fighter; a man that never complained. It was a devastating time for them all. The loss was a very great one and all they could do was to take it one day at a time. One night I had a dream about Debbie's Dad. He had been flying in the sky. The sky was the crispest blue I have ever seen and there were fluffy white clouds. He was flying on a mountain top where the whole mountain was covered in dark green pine trees. He was saying "I am free, I can fly, and I am great". It was absolutely beautiful. In the dream he then flew to his granddaughter Crystal's bedroom where he placed a quilt on her bed. I went to work and told Debbie about this the next day. We validated her dad was saying I am free, I can fly, I feel great – I am no longer confined to a wheel chair. Debbie also validated that Crystal had taken her grandfather's quilt from his bed and put it on hers. I believe it was her grandfather saying I want you to have this and to let her know he knew she had taken the quilt and that made him very happy.

A few years later when Debbie's Mom passed she told me her sign to her granddaughter Sharisse were butterflies. Sharisse came to one of my message evenings where her grandmother came through to say thank you for holding my hand in death. They had a strong spiritual bond. I also said she was making a wind chime move and with that we heard wind chimes in the room! (There were no physical wind chimes in the room) We heard them three times that night. Her grandmother was happy Sharisse had bought her house as she would love it and look after it. A few months later she came in a dream to say she was happy that the house was warm and she was by a fireplace. I emailed Debbie to tell her this and she confirmed that Sharisse had just bought a fireplace for her house! Later Sharisse sent me a video of a butterfly shadow dancing on her fireplace.

I felt fortunate to have worked in the bank where I connected to many wonderful people. Some knew I was a medium and some not. Some still have no idea as this was not something I spoke about very often. But word gets out and some would ask me to do readings for them. One day Corrie came in to the bank to let me know her Dad had passed away. She just needed to cry and she knew I would hug her so I did. That evening I had a dream about her Dad that he had done everything he had wanted to do on earth. He was at the end of his learning lessons and he was very much at peace. Corries Dad came through in this most amazing presence – like an angel. I have never felt so much peace and tranquillity in all my life. It was truly amazing. He just wanted Corrie to know he was ok and he had evolved to a really high level. When he was around her she would feel a whole sense of peace. I really felt the angelic realm. I called Corrie to let her know of my dream and she was so happy to hear that her Dad was ok and that he evolved to such a high level and he would be her guardian angel now.

In another dream I had Joanne's Dad Phillip appear to me. Joanne and her husband Craig were at the bank paying off some debts. Joanne was asking me when it was all going to get paid out as it was supposed to be done on the first of the month. The first was a Sunday so I told her it would be paid out Monday morning. Joanne said it better be paid by 7 a.m. Phillip appeared and told Joanne things happen when they are meant to and you have to let go of any need for control. Phillip showed his son and daughter in law arguing and told Joanne not to worry about them or anyone else as she needed to concentrate on herself and her family. When I told Joanne about this dream she was amazed as they had been at the bank the day before paying off debts and her brother and sister-in-law were indeed arguing! "Wow Dad sure does know what is going on and is watching over us isn't he?"

There is also something I call travelling dreams. I often get messages from people to say "you were in my dreams helping me last night". The most recent one was from Donna saying "My husband was in a room full of demons; they were all around him trying to get to him – then you came into the room and shone your light on them and they vanished. You had no fear of them."

Ellie said I was in her dreams talking about Chakra's which she knew nothing about. I was talking about three colours in particular. I started to tell her about the blue, throat chakra; she started crying and tried to hold back the tears but I told her to let them all out. I told Ellie what I thought was going on with her and she confirmed this was true.

We are all connected as one. We are all multi-dimensional beings and that is why I could be in my bed asleep and be in someone else's dreams at the same time. I have had dreams where I am in three or more places at the same moment. One night I was aware I was in my human body in my bed; at the same moment my grandmother came to me and showed me a lifetime where her and I were men rowing a canoe on a dirty river for charity (although it was called something else in that dimension); at the same time my spirit was at the bottom of my stairs and all these men in spirit form were coming down the stairs; the first person I could make out was my grandfather who said "Wendy we are all multi-dimensional beings; we are everywhere at once". I woke up thinking if I can do that in my dreams I can do that on earth. I expanded my energy into oneness – out into the universes – I felt complete and whole. This is how we should feel at all times; when we separate ourselves from oneness that is when we will have lower vibrational emotions.

A few days after the dream of my grandfather saying we are everywhere at once – I was in the car with Alan when I saw two suns side by side in the sky both moving towards each other until one went behind the other. I recall thinking "yes an earthly validation; there is more than one world!" I shouted to Alan "look can you see this". Alan is a logical person and does not visually see beyond the veil but yes he saw it!

Spirit comes through in wondrous ways. I cannot control how they come through I can only pass the message on in the way they want them to come through. Some people want them to come through in a specific way – how about let go and just allow the message to come, when you do you will get so much more.

Our souls – our beings leave our bodies at night and connect to whoever needs it; we are all interconnected – we are all one.

Try this meditation: Sit quietly, eyes closed. See your being as a beautiful white light inside of you… expand it so it fills up your whole body… keep growing this light until it fills up the room and goes up to the sky… now see the light of the love source energy coming towards you, bright and beautiful… now allow your light and the light of the love source energy to blend together so you can't tell the difference. Now expand that light energy up higher into the sky, allow this light to expand outwards and all around you… now take it higher… going higher than you have ever been before. I want you to tune into your feelings, feel the peace of being in this space, feel the expansion of your energy… you might feel like you are floating or flying, just enjoy being here.

This is an exercise you can do daily. Here's the truth when you are in this high vibration of energy – there is no illness, there is no pain, there is no sadness, no anger or any other negative emotion. There is no separation; only peace and oneness.

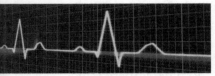

Chapter 11
Princess Diana

I have had a few dreams of Princess Diana over the years. One was shortly after her death where she was visiting lots of people and she was saying she was still with her boys they were her most precious jewels in life. I wondered why I would have a dream of her as I had never had the privilege of meeting her face to face in this life time. I loved Princess Diana for her caring and compassionate ways. I felt very sad at the time of her death for her boy's sake and all that mourned her in the world.

A few years later I had another dream of Princess Diana she was wearing a beautiful light blue gown and a tiara. The tiara was very different it was half diamonds and half made of blue Wedgewood china. I felt the crown represented the two sides of Diana. I remember thinking I had never seen a crown like this before but there was a message in that for her sons. We were in a grand building somewhere in England. The hall ways were wide the carpets patterned with little triangles on them and a stripe down the side by the wall, the wall paper was patterned and there were valuable paintings on the walls, the frames were the colour of gold. With that Prince William walked around the corner, he had wanted to get away from people for a minute and he was all by himself. I went up to him and told him I was a medium and his Mum was with him. He was a very nice person and was interested in what his Mum wanted to say. His Mum started to tell him that he needs to eat properly and she gave him an apple cut into quarters; "sometimes when you are busy you can't always eat so it is important for you to have little snacks." She told him that she was proud of whom he was becoming and that he had the best of both his Mum and Dad in him; they were both good people. I felt Diana's love for everyone in her heart and there really was no malice at all; only love especially for her sons.

A later dream where Princess Diana appeared was around the wedding of Prince William and Kate, Diana was showing me she was there. Again I would wonder why I was having these dreams of her and what I would do with this information, it was not like I could phone them up and say hey I had a dream of your Mum. As anything I do trust it is for a reason and I will know why at a later date.

One time Princess Diana appeared with Prince Harry. She told me that Prince Harry really missed her and carried sadness in his heart; he does not always know what to do with his emotions. She just stood there with her arm around her son with such love and admiration for the good heart he has and for carrying on her caring ways.

Another dream she was lying on a four poster bed stretched out in a lovely short silk dress; she had two more dresses beside her; one of wide green, orange and white strips and another silk one. She said she still loved the designs of Versace. In this dream she was smiling and happy and saying she was changing protocol through her boys.

In the latest one she showed me one of her past lives. She had been a man of royalty who lived in London, England. She had been gambling in a small dark room with other members of high society. She had thirteen hundred pounds on her and she gambled until 7 a.m. she lost one thousand pounds as she only had three hundred pounds left in the morning. This was indeed a lot of money for the lifetime she had been in. She knew she would be in deep trouble if she were to be found out. Diana had been a man in this life time and had taken a little girl with her (him) to the gambling room. After as they were walking along the Thames somewhere she went into a small round tower building with an arch and told the little girl she would have to blow up the tower to destroy any evidence. She told me in this life time she had been balancing out her karma and that is why she corrected herself and had a passion for the landmines in Bosnia. Today there are no land mines in Bosnia, hugely thanks to Princess Diana.

I do believe that one day I will get to say this to Princess Diana's sons whom she loved with all she had.

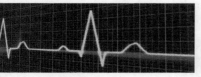

Chapter 12
There is a Treasure in Every Moment

A spirit came through to tell me to look for the treasure in every moment. He had passed life by, he was always looking for money, trying to make money, and trying to have more material things in life like fast cars and fancy houses, after all that is what someone told him he needed in order to be "successful". He was always chasing when meanwhile there were treasures all around him, in front of him every day, in every moment that he did not always see.

There were the good times he had spent with family and friends; there were treasures in the messages all around him. There were beautiful colours he could see at all times, but he was too busy looking at what he did not have to appreciate it all. Once he accomplished one thing he wanted something else – nothing was ever enough for him! He had never been content with enjoying the moment.

He loved to hunt and fish but was never happy unless he caught something – he forgot about the treasure in the quietness, the crunch of the snow underfoot, the beautiful sun rises. No he was someone who had a chip on his shoulder and thought the world owed him more. He wanted material things; things he had to leave behind. It is not the material possessions that will make a difference to your soul when you leave this world; things that do not matter when you die. Joey wished he had enjoyed every day more than he had.

So look around you now as there are many treasures right under your very nose – you do not have to go far to see them or feel them, just appreciate every single one of them and when you do more will appear.

Joey took his loved ones for granted here on earth as many do. For you reading this book today take a moment to thank your loved ones around you for being here, for making a difference. Some people complain and even shout at their loved ones and say mean things but just take a moment and ask yourself how would you feel if they were gone? It is human nature that our brains are wired differently here on earth but try switching your thinking to what is great about this person? What do I love most about them? What can I do to help them appreciate more? How can I be a contribution to them? How can I help change their perception? How can I change my perception? How can I love them more?

What would make you happier in this very moment? Appreciate nature and all of its glory as it is truly a gift. Appreciate and be thankful for all you have as this opens your heart to more love; gratitude is a beautiful thing when you truly feel it.

Something you can do is get a journal or notepad and write "what I am grateful for". Everyday write something; starting from the moment you get out of bed – be grateful for your bed; running water; food; a roof over your head; electricity; whatever you think. Keep adding to your list. If you have someone that you are not getting on with – write down what is good about that person; even if you can only think of one thing – maybe they are a good gardener. Write down what you are learning from them and be grateful for it all. If you have days where you feel sorry for yourself – pick up your gratitude journal and read it.

"If you aren't happy for what you already have then what makes you think you will be happy with more – virtues have a far greater value than the material things".

Life is for living; it is a true experience; so explore and have fun doing it. Thank you for sharing this Joey and for making a difference in this wonderful world full of amazing treasures.

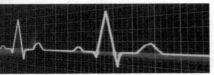

Chapter 13
One Moment in Time

As I sit here listening to "One Moment in time" by Whitney Houston spirits descend upon me. I love this song it really connects to me bringing up so much emotion. I think to myself who do I want to spend one moment in time with today that has passed? I wanted my Gran on my Mums side to come sit with me, but sometimes we don't always get what we want we get what we need. My Grandmother on my Dads side appeared; I really only have one living memory of her; I was told she loved all her grandchildren so very much. Even so I wanted my other Gran to come in.

When my youngest daughter was about eighteen months old and we were cuddling on the couch, she pointed to the ceiling and said "look! There's Great Grandma." I replied which one as three had died at that time. She said "you know the one who lived on the farm with the cows and the chickens and she had a dog." That was my Dad's Mum I thought it was lovely that my daughter was so open to be able to see her. I knew at that moment she had met her great grandmother before she was born and it was my Grannies way of telling me.

So today she is appearing before me. I accept that she is here and not my other Gran. During our connection I wanted to go and sit on a park bench but instead she took me to a duck pond. I let go the control and went with her. I saw myself aged two years old; we were feeding the ducks together. It was like I was above my body just viewing this. I would throw the ducks some bread and when the ducks ate it I would do a belly laugh as children do, it made me laugh just to observe this. How magical that I could feel that belly laugh again, how wonderful it was to have this moment with my Grannie. I laughed and laughed and laughed! How lucky I am to be so open to this other world. I thanked my Grannie, forever grateful that I can still see her and have a relationship with her. Grateful that my Grannie had been aware I had been too serious and needed to laugh and have fun. My Grannie gave me the laughter I needed. My energy felt light and free after I had spent those few minutes with her in meditation. I cannot force the other world or force myself to see; whoever wants to share a message with me will. Whoever wants to channel a message through me will do so. I feel blessed by the love and guidance I receive. Grateful for one moment in time!

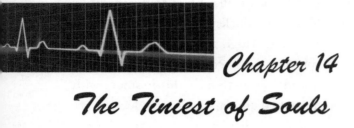

Chapter 14
The Tiniest of Souls

Amongst the darkest nights the tiniest of souls is conceived, it sets alight the smallest flame, a flame of love, of hope and all the promises to come. That tiniest of soul can cause so much excitement and anticipation for what the future may hold.

Then from nowhere that tiniest flame can go out, without warning, for reasons unknown to us.

Before we even have a chance to meet that tiny soul, they can be taken from us, but not before they leave their tiny imprint on our heart. Never to be removed. They might have the tiniest of flame but they know enough to light other flames and leave the world a better place. They shared their love. We may think they have the smallest of hearts but actually it is quite the opposite. The biggest of hearts are conceived, they show us how much love we can have even though we have not met in the physical sense. Our spirits meet and we connect to unconditional love. When you love unconditionally with no attachments, no expectations, that love grows and grows. They can teach us so much in such a short time; sometimes more than someone you have known for many years that have lived here on earth. It is amazing the difference one tiny heartbeat can make. To the little souls who chose to be here for only a short time ; thank you; thank you for sharing the biggest of hearts. Thank you for lighting the way with all your love.

May you keep the flame burning and keep lighting the flames of others, sharing your love and experiences with them.

I was preparing for a message evening one afternoon. I put some music on to prepare for my one moment in time with loved ones in heaven when a little baby was placed in my arms. I thought someone coming tonight has lost babies and they will come through for their Mum. I felt the need to put something on my face book page about this experience. As the same time I was typing the message on face book I received a message from someone named Jessica asking me what my thoughts were on something that just happened to her. She was at work with some co-workers in their lunch room when a tiny bubble appeared from the ceiling. It went passed her and landed on the table. I told Jessica she had lost the tiniest of spirits and this was their sign to her. They wanted her to know they were still around and wanted her to have fun with bubbles. Jessica told me she had lost two tiny souls recently and that she had just purchased a bubble machine for her three year old daughter, so tonight she was going to have fun with bubbles. I told her that it was a validation for her. Those little souls had a purpose of bringing more love into this world even for that short time they had a big impact on people already. For their Mum, more love and understanding that even the tiniest of souls stick around. For the little soul's sister Imogen they would be around her, playing with her. For myself, more understanding to write this chapter. Those tiniest of souls inspired me, bought me clarity so that others can read this and understand that although we don't know why these things happen, it can give us a little insight and a whole lot more love to be thankful for.

At the message evening that night there were indeed little souls coming through. One had let his Mum know that it was indeed the wrong time for him to come into this world and that is why he opted out – he would be born to her again in two years' time in another little boy.

As I was doing a reading for Bianca she had two baby spirits come through with her. They told her not to carry the burden around of her choice to abort them. She had split from her relationship which left her with two young children. She had become pregnant twice due to different circumstances and inside she knew the best thing for everyone would be to abort them. The babies had come through to let her know that they were both boys and through them she would learn judgement. One of them would stay with her in spirit for the rest of time while one would come back to her a few years later. This indeed did happen when she was in a relationship and she gave birth to a beautiful little boy. Every situation is different and many people judge without knowing the whole story. Even if they do know it every single person is different and must make the right choice for them and no one else.

When Emma came to see me I could see a tiny soul with her. I could tell this was a little girl for Emma. The reason she lost that baby was so that she could protect her brother here on Earth. She could play with him and always be there for him. She would help him with his schooling and help him to read. She would be his teacher in spirit.

Sometimes the tiniest of spirits are strong enough to get their messages through to their parents through others. I was doing a group reading and a young soul appeared called Grace. She wanted to thank her Mum for the balloon. One of the girls in the group said that was her neighbour's daughter and as soon as the readings were over she would go straight home and tell her neighbour. The neighbour validated the message because that day was Grace's birthday and they had let a balloon free for her to receive in Heaven!

The tiniest of souls all have a special purpose; all making a huge difference on earth and in heaven.

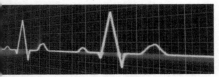

Chapter 15
Loss and Heartache

O n February 3, 2010 my life would forever change. My son Hunter at the young age of only eighteen months old made his journey home to God. The night before was like any other night. Life was busy with four children at home, myself and my soon to be husband. I went about my day as usual, spending most of it worrying about finances, cleaning the house doing laundry and sneaking in the time to play with the kids. By the end of the day I was left feeling like I didn't do enough, or like every other parent in the world, did I do a good job as a parent? My words to my fiancé that night will forever be etched into my body and soul. I said to him "you know I have been home all day and I feel like I have barely seen Hunter" I wanted so bad to go crawl into his bed and sleep with him. Was it mothers intuition or did my soul already know what was coming and started to prepare? Just thinking I was over reacting I crawled into bed and went to sleep for the night.

In the morning when I went to wake my son, he was gone. Life had lost its meaning to me. I was crippled with pain and heart ache. I forgot how to breathe. How was I ever going to survive this, for myself and for my fiancé, but most of all the three sisters Hunter left behind?

Very quickly my life began to change. There was new medication to calm me, some to help me sleep, and even some to try and make me happy again; all while I was struggling to just exist. Then one day I received a message, I was told I needed to see Wendy Terry, I was told she was an amazing medium; the seed had been planted. Within two days I must have heard about Wendy a half a dozen times. So I began to search, I tracked Wendy down at work and called her, from that moment my life would change again.

It started first with just a reading. Wendy was amazing. She told me of how my son still played with his sisters. She explained in detail a little picnic basket she saw him playing with. Well it was just fifteen minutes before that I was watching my daughters play with the exact basket she described back at home. I told her of my white candle that I lit the day Hunter left and weeks later it was still burning. Wendy informed me to burn a yellow candle she said there was healing to be had in the color yellow for me. So I made the switch and waited for the change. Before leaving my reading Wendy reached out to me. She was my angel sent to me from Heaven and offered to work very closely with me to help me through the toughest battle life will ever throw at me. Without hesitation I accepted.

The next time I saw Wendy we did Emotional Freedom Technique (EFT). This is a form of tapping to release emotions from the body. During that time Wendy would relay messages from my son. One of which was that it was time to blow out my candle. I was using the candle as a security blanket and needed to work through the emotion of letting go. The most profound words were said to me that day with Wendy, she told me "Misty, you need to let go of your guilt, and you need to forgive yourself, because if you had any control over the matter you know you never would have let this happen." She also told me to watch for ladybugs; Hunter was going to send them in every form, on cards, in pictures and even live ones. I left my session with Wendy that day feeling more free and alive than I had in a few weeks. I proceeded to flush my medication down the toilet and not look back. I knew in my heart Wendy was giving me the tools I needed to get through this. Later that night it was the first time I bathed my kids, played with my kids and genuinely laughed with my kids since Hunters passing. Just before putting my girls to bed that night we found a ladybug flying around the kitchen in February! (We had had snow for four months already in Canada). The next morning I was working up the courage to go blow out my candle that had been lit for weeks, when I got to it the candle was out. The fear I had about the one breathe I needed to blow out the candle was gone. Some way, somehow, I don't know if it was my son or the angels, or an act of God but the candle was out and I didn't have to go through the pain and emotions to do it myself.

My time spent with Wendy would bring so many more lessons and life changing messages. I took the time I needed to grieve and release. Had it not been for the healing messages of love Wendy Terry brought through to me, I honestly can tell you I would still be lost and full of grief. Wendy gave me back the tools I needed to learn to breathe again. She paved the path all the while lining it with flowers so I could stop for a moment and smell the roses when living got to be too much.

Now six years later, I still am comforted by yellow, yellow candles, yellow flowers, and yellow skies. I still watch for lady bugs and send my son love and light every time I see one. Though I have dealt with the grief, it is still a scar I wear proudly. People say time heals, I disagree. Time teaches us to better cope with the loss and heart ache. The one thing I know for sure is, if that loss and heart ache was not there that would mean Hunter was never really here, and the short eighteen months I got to spend with Hunter is so worth the life time of heart ache I will have missing him.

– Misty Scott

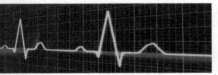

Chapter 16

Pedestal

L orna knew I was a medium and had called to say that her son Chris had just lost his best friend. Travis had died in a vehicle accident on a slippery winter's day in Manitoba, Canada. There was a dangerous s curve in the road and he had died instantly. He left behind a shock wave for his family and friends to cope with. Travis was the tender age of seventeen and was in his senior year of high school. That fatal December day will always be imbedded on their minds.

Lorna asked if I would go to see the family and see if I could help them. I told her there were no guarantees he would come through especially seeing he had only past away a few months before. Lorna said she would meet me there and introduced me to his family, Wayne, Francis, Robin and Peter. Wayne did not believe in any of this and sat in the living room while we all sat around the kitchen table. Wayne wanted to listen but not be too close.

Travis came through the minute I had entered the house, his presence very strong. He was so happy that his family were there. The family were originally from Newfoundland, somewhere I had not been before. Travis began showing me images and described a restaurant. It was an old fashioned 50's diner with a rock 'n roll jukebox and tables with checked table cloths. Fran replied that it was their favourite restaurant and they would go there often. Travis gave more specific details and his Dad's ears started to prick up. Maybe there was something in this he thought. Travis told his sister he liked the car she had bought the day before. He described it to her and told her to keep it clean! The car was in the garage so there was no way that I could have seen it. He told his Mom that he was moving objects around and taking things from the kitchen. She confirmed that spoons had been disappearing and she would find them in his room! He told his sister Robin not to worry about things disappearing from his room. She had been upset when someone had told Travis' friends they could have his clothes and any of his possessions. His Mom thought this was a good way to help his friends heal from this terrible ordeal. Travis was standing behind Robin at the table and I told her to stand up to feel him. She did and yes she could feel the difference in the energy where he was. Robin had gifts herself and this would help her to open up more. Robin had a very emotional experience but felt better afterwards. Robin confided in me that Travis had come to her in dreams. She was afraid to look at him because his family had part of his eyes donated to help someone else see; Robin thought his image would have no eyes. I explained to Robin that he would appear in a peaceful state with no injuries and be complete. Robin thought he would appear as the spirits shown in the "Ghost Whisper" (a TV series about spirits before they transition to the other side.) Robin felt better, no longer afraid to see her brother.

Fran was very open to everything and Travis knew she would receive and learn so much on her journey ahead. She would be the glue in the family and somehow help them all through this.

Travis told his Dad that he loved his tattoo in his honour. He had indeed had a tattoo of Travis tattooed on his arm. He told his brother Peter that he was smart and needed to advance in school. He was a good mechanic. Travis would guide him in the right direction. Travis came through for his best friend Chris and told him that he would play tricks on him and have fun with him. He did not want anyone to be so serious. Travis was concerned over his Dad. Yes everyone was grieving but his Dad was turning inside. He wanted his Dad to let his anger out to get a punching bag and let loose. His Dad was distancing himself from the family. Wayne had indeed put Travis up on a pedestal – making Travis more important than his other two children. Travis came through to his Dad to say you have two other children here who love you and need you. Yes I know you miss me but they are still alive. They miss you and need you. The family was falling apart! Wayne did not listen and chose to put all his energy and attention on Travis. He had been very proud of Travis as he was the one who continued with the naval reserves while the other two had not. Peter and Robin had pretty well lost faith in their Dad, feeling that they did not matter to him anymore. I went back to the house on another occasion with a friend who was also a psychic and gave them some more messages. This time we picked up on their Nan who presented herself with breathing difficulties. She had in fact died in a house fire from smoke inhalation. The Nan spoke about someone stealing money from her. She described a thirty year old man even down to his clothing. This was all true and they knew there was no way that we would have known that. Wayne and Peter became believers! A short while later I did a reading for Wayne where Travis came through to tell him to mend things with Robin and Peter.

A few years' later Wayne and Fran attended one of my message evenings and Travis came through again. Travis was so happy that the road that he had died on had been straightened and divided with a safety barrier. Improvements that could help prevent future deaths or accidents. Travis thanked his Dad for setting him free and allowing him to go even higher in spirit – to a new level. He was proud of his Dad because he had brought the family back together again. He was listening and paying attention to Robin and Peter. Wayne had proudly walked Robin down the aisle. Travis had been there and watched it. Now this family was stronger than ever.

Travis was a very thoughtful person here on earth so it would make sense that in death he was still thinking of others. His family made it, they became stronger, somehow all pulling together. Other families are not so lucky. So it is Travis' hope that by reading this, it will give other parents a different perspective. Children living on earth are still so important. Travis would like his Dad to add to his tattoo, a picture of his brother and sister for his complete family.

This would be a wonderful way to contribute to the living and the dead – a balance of both realms. All can be honoured and all can be thought of every day.

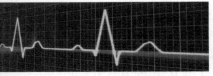

Chapter 17
Magical Fairy

The hardest funeral I ever had to attend was Thora's. At just four years old it was heart wrenching. I personally dread going to funerals as I can feel everyone's pain and emotion so try to stay away. I feel so much for the family. Thora's was an exception; I felt I needed to go to give her family support. I am sure the funeral is now a blur to her family; you are going through grief and shock and there are so many people coming up and hugging you and talking to you.

I remember at Thora's funeral there were many pink and blue balloons and it looked beautiful. I remember watching them and all of a sudden the balloons started moving and I could see Thora playing and having fun with them. She was right there loving them. I could see a gathering of people in spirit above her watching. I knew it was not the day to tell her parents but knew I would go and see them after the funeral, when things had settled down a little. As soon as the funeral service was finished everyone took a balloon in honour of Thora and her birthday and went outside and released them. It was beautiful and emotional at the same time.

A short while after Thora's funeral I went to visit Thora's Mom Kim, who was at home with her son Aidan. He was one at the time and busy playing on the floor. I told Kim that I had seen Thora playing with the balloons during the funeral service and she loved them. I also told her that Aidan would see her because she would come and play with him. Thora was still very much in the home and came at night to give her Mommy butterfly kisses on her cheeks. Thora had died from chronic granulomatous disease something her sister Alida also suffered from. Thora told me that her sister would get sick again and she had gone before her to save her. Her sister still had much to do in this life time and would be working with children. She could write children's books about her experience in the hospital to help other people going through the same thing. Thora told her Mommy she was giving her a rainbow. Her Mom mentioned that Thora's last picture she drew in the hospital and gave to her was of a rainbow. Thora loved to be outside with her Dad Jeff and would "tinker" in the garage with him. Thora loved Tinkerbelle, so it was no surprise that Tinkerbelle's image became her sign to her family. Just like the magical little fairy Thora loves to fly and do good things when her spirit is around them.

Years later Thora still knows when to give her family messages. Just recently before Christmas I decided to Grant Wishes for people to connect to their loved ones in Heaven. I was feeling so blessed and grateful for the connections I have that I wanted to share those gifts with others. I put a message on my face book page "Open Minds with Wendy Terry" that I would be granting wishes and who would like a connection. A couple of people had commented that they would like to give their wish to Kim and her family as they were all generous, loving, giving people. I could see Thora with me saying she wanted to give her family messages so I granted the wish. I made a telephone connection to Kim and her family. Thora came through for each one of them; she gave a specific message to each family member as well as a theme to them for 2018 and a message for the family as a whole. The family were so grateful and said "thank you will never not be enough". They had really needed the message and to hear from Thora.

I know for me personally to this day when Thora is around helping me with children she always shows me at least one Tinkerbelle. If I don't notice it right away she shows me many in a row so I know it is no coincidence. I have seen them everywhere at airports, restaurants, at people's houses; they appear on towels, handbags, clothing, jewellery, and all sorts of things.

Thora was that little soul who saw the magic in everything. She lifted people up by just being around them. She still has the magic to lift people up from where she is – all you have to do is think of her!

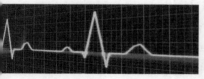

Chapter 18
Happy Birthday

When I was visiting my daughter Mandy and her husband in Thunder Bay Ontario Mandy asked if I could do a reading for her friend Nadia who was having a hard time. When I met Nadia I instantly sensed a huge well of sadness within her so knew there was a close loss around her. I told her that her Mom was with her and she broke down in tears, this was so very hard for her. I gave Nadia some messages from her Mom as well as doing some emotional releasing with her and she felt better; better that her Mom was still around her.

Another time when I was back in Thunder Bay to do a message show I was drawn to buy a gift for someone and put it in a "Happy Birthday bag" I knew it would be someone's birthday at my show. While doing the show I asked "who has a birthday here tonight?" Nadia's sister put up her hand. I told her that I had been drawn to buy this gift and her Mom came through to give her some messages. Her Mom wanted to wish her a Happy Birthday; she was with her always. The timing of my show was close to Christmas and the gift in the bag was a beautiful angel ornament for the Christmas tree. When they opened it they cried because it was an exact replica of one their Mother used to have. Their Mother had loved Christmas and decorated her house to the fullest and every year they would decorate their houses with their mother's ornaments to honour her. That year however Nadia had decided not to decorate her house for Christmas as her father was sick and they were having some troubles with him. This gift reminded them that their Mother wanted them to decorate for Christmas and she was always with them. She was there for their birthdays and gave them the gift of an angel "herself". The next day we had gone to the restaurant where Nadia worked I told her that her Mom still needed me to give her some more messages and she was sending her a blue sparkly butterfly – it was very specific. Nadia wrote to tell me that a couple of months later, when she was having a huge melt down and was crying and screaming she grabbed a travel pillow her Mom had made for her (she kept it on her bed and had slept with it since her Moms death a few years before). She sobbed into the pillow and felt something prickly. She thought it was a feather but when she looked, there staring at her was a beautiful sparkly blue butterfly! She had never noticed it before – it was like it had just appeared. Nadia's Mom was with her in her hour of need and helped her to feel better.

Just before New Year's Eve I had the vision of a male with me he put his daughter Joanne into my mind so I knew it was her Dad Phillip. I messaged Joanne through face book to say "Hi Joanne, I want you to know that your Dad is very strong around me tonight and wanted me to message you. He wants me to wish you a very happy new year. It is like he is walking in front of you to get your attention; he is in your kitchen. You will think you are clumsy but it will be him knocking things out of your hand. Your Dad is holding a birthday cake, he is celebrating with you. He knows you still miss him very much." Joanne messaged back "omg Wendy, my birthday is December 31st and I will be fifty. So glad he came to you as I have been waiting a long time to hear from him. Please let him know that I think of him every day and still miss him so much. Thank you my dear you have made my day and my year". I replied "no wonder he wanted to wish you a happy birthday. That is the best present ever! You see they still know what is going on and that is a validation for you. Happy Birthday and a wonderful New Year to you. Your Dad also wants to thank you for everything you do for your Mom. He sent her a beautiful star at Christmas; hope she saw and caught it". Joanne said she for sure would pass that on to her Mom. "My Dad was very strong here on earth and it just proves he is still that strong in spirit." "Happy 50th Birthday to my dearest Joanne, I would never miss any special days of my family – I am always here." Love Dad xo

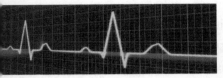

Chapter 19
Piss 'n Vinegar

While doing one of my shows in England I had given Jenny a message from her Mum Frances. Frances had shown me that she used to sit in an easy chair and that it was "her" chair. Jenny's Mum lived with her and had been sick in the end. Her Mum wanted Jenny to throw the chair out now that she was gone as it had her magnetic imprinting on it, the energy of her sickness; it was time for her to let go. Now sometimes spirit makes me swear at shows as that is how they want to come through and I have to trust it. I told Jenny her Mums saying was "you are full of piss 'n vinegar". It is a saying you do not hear any more and I am sure many people have never heard of it. I was not sure but I trusted it and said it and Jenny understood completely. She said that it was indeed something that her Mother would say. Even Jenny's friend had to question if it was true as she had never heard of that saying before.

I told her to look for the saying as her Mum would be sending that message about piss 'n vinegar to her. (Even for me I think how is she going to do that, but again I follow their energy in telling me what to say) A few months later Jenny informed me that she had gone on a bus trip for a holiday and someone had given her a book to read along the way. As she was reading it she read the words "you are full of piss 'n vinegar." She immediately thought of her Mum and the words I had told her; something made her look at the book title as she had not even taken notice of it. The book was called "Angel" by Barbara Taylor Bradford. She was so taken aback and surprised but felt very comforted as now she knew her Mum was on the trip with her.

I could see her Mum with her and told her that your Mum is full of piss 'n vinegar right now. She has a real twinkle in her eye and is being mischievous; something she had lost in the end of her life time here from being sick. Frances told Jenny to get out more; you need more play; you work too much; try to get out more and join a group and have fun. I know it is not easy when you have worked all day but you can do something on a weekend or you day off. Jenny understood what she meant. Then Jenny went back to talking about the book with the message in it and said I even remember the page number, it was 293. I said there is a message in that I had Doreen Virtues book Daily Guidance from Your Angels. I looked up the message under 293 and it was "Balance Play and Work". The piss 'n vinegar was about that, having fun and playing! We really do receive messages in all ways.

Chapter 20

Funny Spirits

Spirits can be very funny at times. If someone was a joker on earth they can often come through with the same energy. I was doing a message evening when Bridie's dad Trevor came through for her. He was telling her he was moving and hiding things all over her house to be funny, she said that would be him. Trevor also gave her a message about sausages and he made me laugh. At the time Bridie was not quite sure what it was about. Sometimes we have to piece the puzzle together. I have to raise my energy to meet the spirits energy; they usually have to lower their energy so we can connect and I can then be the medium. Sometimes the line can be static and depending on who I am giving the reading for, they can be resistant to receiving the message. Sometimes this can be from fear or maybe they are skeptical. Over the years I have said a few things to people, even told them names of people they did not know, only for them to come back to me and say I know who that is now. Bridie was just caught off guard in receiving such a funny message but later that night she messaged me to say I get the sausage message now! Yesterday while I was at work I wanted sausages and the chef hid them away from me. It took me at least ten minutes to find them. It was actually Bridie's Dad hiding them on her and having fun with her. He just put what he wanted into the mind of the chef. He was telling her he was still having fun with her and loved it when she laughed.

When I messaged Bridie to get permission to use this in the book she told me that her Dad had come through for her daughter Bella who was four years old. Luckily Bridie knows enough to keep her daughter open and ask questions like what is he wearing? Or what is he saying? Bella told her Mum that her Granddad came through and he was wearing a hat with feathers. This would go with Trevor's personality of being funny as he wanted to tickle her and make her laugh. I had told Bridie previously that her Dads sign were feathers and the day I told her she had said that she had been out with Bella and they had found feathers everywhere. Bella said her Granddad lives in heaven and that it is glowy up there. She said to her Mum he can disappear; her Mum asked "how do you know that?" Bella replied "because sometimes he takes me with him". Bella had seen heaven; she described it as glowy and beautiful.

Many children are so open to this realm and if you have a child around that can see or know about this realm then I would encourage you to keep them open even if you don't understand it all. It is important to laugh and have fun; Trevor loves to see his daughter and granddaughter having fun. He loves it when Bella does a real belly laugh or squeals with delight as this makes him laugh with them.

Some spirits like to trip you up as they think that is really funny! Mike in spirit loves to trip me and my friends up. Once when I was in Canada walking out of a restaurant after having breakfast with a couple of friends, I tripped on the way to the parking lot. I could feel someone's hand on me as I did a full summersault and landed back on my feet. Well it was like this happened in slow motion! I still burst out laughing as I think of this. My friends Tammie and Jeneen were with me and afterwards they bust a gut (as we would say in Canada). Someone driving by stopped to see if I was ok – I was and like I said all we could do was laugh! We literally spent the whole day laughing. Mike is always around me making me laugh. Mike has been passed away for over twenty years but he is very much around – he was the funniest person that I had ever met on the earthly plane. I am grateful he can still make me laugh like no one else. I also know that when they trip you up they will also always make sure you are ok and you don't hurt yourself.

Think of a funny spirit with you today and laugh with them!

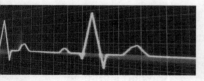

Chapter 21
Papi's Help

Marta arrived in Canada from Venezuela to start university. Her father had wanted her to better herself. Marta studied language and after a year while on holiday she met her future husband. Marta decided to move to Selkirk, Manitoba with him and began a life there. Marta started working at the bank where I worked and I instantly took her under my wing. Sometimes there is just an instant connection with someone you meet right away. Maybe it was because I knew Marta had no family here and I wanted to extend my love to her. A few years down the line Marta's marriage fell apart and she went on to have another relationship. During this relationship Marta fell pregnant. She confided in me and said she wanted to have the baby as she thought at the age of twenty six this would be the only child she would have. The baby's father at that time decided to back off as he was in a complicated relationship. I told Marta that if she wanted the baby I would be there for her and be her coach. We went to prenatal classes together and I was there when her wonderful son Fabian was born. It was an incredible experience and definitely bonded us even closer. I admired Marta's strength and courage for becoming a single mother. When Fabian was six months old Marta took him to Venezuela to meet her Dad – her Papi. How he loved Fabian who was so fair and blue eyed like him. Fabian got to be loved and spoilt by Marta's whole family.

Upon returning to Selkirk Marta had a hard time. It was very hard for her to be away from her family. It was hard for her to return to work and hard for her to meet the bills. She lived in an apartment that had iron steps so could be slippery in winter. She had a vehicle that was always breaking down – not a good thing when you have a baby. A few months after returning from Venezuela she had the devastating news that her Papi had passed away. Although she was very happy that her Papi got to meet Fabian she was so upset.

While I was at her place one day her Papi came through in spirit. I told her that he was saying "I can help you more now I am here. I will watch over you both and make sure you are ok."

Well a few weeks later Marta was looking for a van because her old car was caput and a van was easier with a one year old. Someone offered her a van that was very much in her price bracket. I told her it was from her Dad, he sent her a reliable vehicle. After that it seemed that the baby's father was starting to come around more and wanted to see more of Fabian and Marta. Next there was a job promotion for Marta with more hours and more pay. She was able to start saving as she wanted somewhere better for her and her son to live.

After working things out with Fabians' dad he moved in with them. Then sadly his grandfather passed away but they were now able to buy his house trailer which was so much bigger than their apartment. Things had definitely improved for Marta since her Papi had passed away.

Many times spirit can do more for us after they have passed than when they were living. It is a good practise to ask them for help.

To *Papi*

Thank you for your wise advice and all your life lessons to me. I'm forever grateful to have you for my father. You showed me to be free, to love and appreciate nature, to love others and to stand up for my beliefs, to be honest and follow my heart.

The last time we spoke we were terribly afraid it would be our last. We both needed you to stay alive; there was still so much you needed to teach me. There was Fabian who you loved and were so proud of, you needed to stay to see him grow up.

But God called you to heaven and after a while of your body not being present I understood you were still with me, you were still close to me. You continued showing me the way and showing us your love.

Now I see you smile and your heart fill with pride when you look at Fabian. You always said he was your replacement and I see you in him every day, your strength, your wisdom, your passionate soul. I see you in him.

– A grateful daughter, Marta

Chapter 22
Guiding Spirits

Many years ago I looked at my husband as he stood in the kitchen and saw a man standing with him and described him. He said it sounded like his grandfather who had died before I met him.

My husband and I were having a discussion as he had a chance to go to Norway with his work for six weeks to work and learn with some people from all over the world in his field of work. We had three children to consider our youngest only being four at the time. We decided he would go as it was such a great opportunity for him. His Nana lived in England and was elderly and had been diagnosed with breast cancer so we knew she would not have long to live. I told him that he should stop and see her on his way to Norway which he did. Four weeks later I got a phone call from him to say that the people in Norway had wanted him to actually stay on for another two weeks! I was not happy with this as the girls and I were missing him and I felt like there was a lot on my plate at home. He asked if I would come for the two weeks as they would pay for my airfare. As much as this would be nice I could not leave the girls as

I was there anchor at that time, their Dad had been gone for four weeks already, I could not up and leave them too.

A day later he called and said how would I feel if they paid for us all to go? I said my bags are packed!

I had the privilege of meeting my husband's Nana on our honeymoon. I instantly connected with her and loved her. Her only great grandchildren were those in Canada and she longed to meet them. So while making our flight plans I had the urge to do a stopover in England on the way back so the girls could meet their great Nana even if it were only for a few days. We had an amazing time in Norway and an even greater time when the girls met their Great Nana. She was so happy and loved them. We took many treasured photos. One evening we started to look through her photo's when the man I saw with my husband stared back at me – it was indeed his grandfather. I know he guided us and put things in place so his wife could meet her beloved great grandchildren; something we did not have the money for at that time. This was the first time the plane stopped in London it usually stopped in Europe – coincidence? I think not! We will always be forever grateful to him for giving us all such a treasured gift. When Great Nana died three months later although it bought sadness I felt a great sense of peace around her.

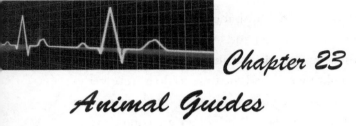

Chapter 23
Animal Guides

Sixteen year old Loren attended one of my shows along with her parents. In the break one of the guests had accidentally spilt their drink; I noticed that Loren cleaned the drink up for her without being asked. I am lead by spirit to bring little gifts that they often want the audience members to receive and I was told to give Loren the "angel of kindness" that I had on the table. I thanked Loren for being so kind; pretty special for a sixteen year old to clean something up without being asked. As I was giving her the angel I could see a hamster appear with her over her shoulder. I told Loren she had a hamster with her and he was helping her to make a decision. I told her she had lots of animals with her as well as Saint Frances (the patron saint of animals). I said to Loren "you must love animals as the hamster is telling you that you should work with them as you are so kind; it is your kindness and caring ways that are your strengths. The hamster is helping you make a decision with what you want to do with your life." Loren confirmed that she had a few animals that had passed and it was her hamster that had upset her the most. She was happy for the hamster to come through. At the end of the show Loren's Dad confirmed she was making a decision as to be a vet or to be an architect – I know what the hamster wants her to do!

While doing a reading for Louise her cat Jackson came through for her; I could hear a very deep wise voice talking to me from the cat. The cat had indeed had lifetimes of being human; he was giving Louise wisdom and knowledge. Jackson was now going to be her guide. Louise definitely had a connection with this lovely cat and had been very close to him while he lived on earth. The next time I worked with Louise her other cat Jazzman came through with her to help with healing; both special cats with different ways; both equally as important as they help Louise as she evolves on her journey.

You can have animals you have had in this life time come through as well as an animal spirit guide (an animal you have not known while doing this earthly journey). Six years ago I had a dream of my grandfather and he told me he was bringing me a new spirit animal – He gave me the most amazing unicorn. The unicorn told me "I am giving you strength so you can keep moving forward on your journey." The unicorn stood looking at me; the sky in the background of where he was. The sky was white with bright orange and bright pink with a streak of grey in the middle. The unicorn said "Keep charging ahead, you will have some obstacles but jump over them and try not to go through them; even if you knock a few down it will be ok". He continued "the colour pink means love – to love yourself and love others; love every situation as you learn from them all. The white is about new beginnings and to keep centred between the worlds. The orange is for creativity, new pieces are opening up, it also means to keep connected to your sexuality and to be proud of whom you are. The grey is for the confusion when you get disconnected. There are times when you will lose your way and you will have to battle the obstacles as your strength will fall away – it won't be major as you will find your way back and regain your strength and clarity." I was grateful to my grandfather for this new spirit animal. We are all shown things when we are ready to see, listen and receive. A few days later I received a gift of a large white male unicorn (he looked like the one in my dream – no coincidences as I did not pay much attention to them before my dream) he now sits proudly on my mantel as he watches over me.

Animals are amazing creatures; you can receive many messages through them. If you ever receive a birthday card with an animal on it or if you see an animal look the meaning of it up – I love the book "Animal Spirit Guides" by Steven D. Farmer, Ph.D.

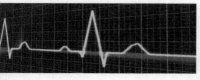

Chapter 24

Jesus

Years ago while doing a telephone reading from my home I felt a presence stand behind me as I was sitting at my desk. This man looked like Jesus, but how could it be Jesus working with me? I felt this intense gold energy penetrate through the back of me into my heart and out of my heart through the phone line to my client. There was so much love here that unless you witness this you will not know this amazing feeling as a human. Wow was all I could think. I thought why would Jesus work with me? I believed in God but I was not religious. I did not like to go to church especially when I heard you had to do things a certain way. I wanted my girls to go to Sunday school so they could make the choice for themselves just as I had. As a family we decided to go to church so my two eldest girls could go to Sunday school. Both girls had been baptised at the church where we went. We had wanted my youngest to be baptised at the same church. We had a beautiful family christening gown which was eighty years old and wanted our youngest daughter to be baptised while the gown still fit her. My husband was scheduled to go away with his work so we needed her to get baptised as soon as possible. When we asked if she could get baptised the church all of a sudden said no because we were not members. Well if going to church every Sunday did not make you a member then I do not know what would. We promised to become official members after my husband got home from his work away but no they would not baptise my daughter. We went to another church that welcomed her with open arms and baptised her. That is what I love about this church unconditional love no matter who you are or where you come from. It was the same church just in a different location. The priest said "I will never turn away a child, if the town drunk came to me then I would say there is hope." He was an amazing man who made a great impact on me. He was kind, gentle and compassionate. Later when my church found out I had my daughter baptised in another church they put in a grievance against that priest. Hence that church was no longer a fit for my belief of unconditional love and acceptance.

I believed Jesus loved and accepted everyone and somehow he wanted me to spread love, something I have always felt even as a little girl. I remember that I loved everyone; we were all the same and I could see no difference. It was not until I was a little older that I would become tainted by other people's belief systems; I heard words like "they are poor", "they are dirty", "they are rich", "don't play with them they are smelly", "they are snobs", "they are mean". It is only in the last two decades that I have learnt to embrace everyone again as I remember we are all one. I truly mean what I say when I appreciate every single person and situation here on earth as I know I am meant to learn something from it remembering we all come from love.

When I was doing emotional releasing on a client of mine the image of Jesus appeared with her. Jesus came through to say "I am not about religion I am about love". I thought yes Jesus helped thousands he did not care who you were or where you came from;

he did not even care what your religion was. Jesus just loved, and gave, and loved some more. Jesus was working through my client also, so she could be the "golden angel" spreading her love and light with her healing hands onto others.

Jesus still continues to spread his light and love through so many others today. Jesus was a master of spreading love, a lesson many have to learn today.

How can you spread some love today?

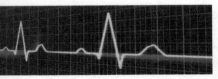

Chapter 25

Goddess Energy

When doing a reading for Hannah her great grandfather on her Dad's side appeared. He had the lack of vibration (fear based) and had passed it down the blood line to Hannah. I could see him burying his money in the back garden, so even though he had a lot of money he was in the lack of vibration. He was afraid someone would take his money and he would be left with nothing. He died with that money still buried in his garden, he was afraid to tell anyone where it was in case they took some; this was his secret and security. No one in his family benefited from any of his hard earned money as it was left to rot in the ground.

I helped Hannah release the lack of vibration back through her ancestor line so she no longer had to carry this with her in this life time.

I could see a beautiful goddess with Hannah; this energy really did make you feel abundant. I told Hannah she was making many sacrifices on this earth but they were for the greatest good of all.

I told her when she died her soul would evolve into this amazing goddess energy and she would be the goddess of abundance, who would be able to help people here on earth and in other realms. The Goddess Realm is a higher level on the other side.

Hannah said "why me?" I said "why not you?" It is not about the brain it is about the heart, you are so kind and caring and you have a heart of gold. This is what you are learning about in this next phase of your life. You are not meant to be like your family and live with their beliefs, they served them well for their time line here on earth but it does not serve your time line. You are meant to expand and learn new things beyond what you think are capable. You are meant to help people on a daily basis by just giving through your heart. This is not always "wow" things. Hannah had mentioned that just that day she had said to someone "Thank you, kind sir". The man was taken aback and said he had not been called sir for a very long time, she had made his day. Yes she had made this man so happy that it increased his vibration and he in turn would do something kind for someone else.

I told Hannah she was learning unconditional love and this was indeed a high quality for the human to learn on this earthly plane. Most human's judge which is a lower vibration and is not unconditional love. She told me she was training to be a midwife; what better way to be around unconditional energy; babies are truly amazing beings as they are open to receiving and giving unconditional love so this made sense in that it would take Hannah to a new level of unconditional love and abundance. Something she can evolve to so when she chooses to die her energy can go to the level of the abundance goddess.

Life if not always what it seems so as much as Hannah was going through hardship; she learnt it belonged to her ancestors so therefore it could be released back to their energy. Hannah can go higher in her vibration so she can learn unconditional love which she needs for her souls purpose so she can work with the goddess energy when she leaves this earth.

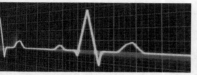

Chapter 26
Presents from Heaven

S pirits can arrange that even though they are in another dimension they can still get a present to you if they want. While talking to Leanne through Face book, she asked about her friend's son Robert. I tuned into his energy and began to give her messages about him. Then Robert mentioned his Mom and wanted to give her some messages. He mentioned that winter was his favourite time of year, especially the first snow fall when there were big snowflakes. He said that his sign to his Mom was a snowflake – especially one that sparkled. Leanne said she would look for one for his Mom. I told her she would not have to look far or hard as it would just appear to her. In the morning when I went on to Face book Leanne had sent me a message to say that as soon as we had disconnected our chat she turned on the TV and there was an advert on about a snowflake. She investigated to find out it was a sparkling Pandora snowflake charm called "Winters Kiss" – a perfect gift from a son to his Mom. Robert wanted his Mom to have something from him and he knew that his Moms friend Leanne who had connected to him was the one who would get it for him.

He in turn would provide the money to her in some way! Merry Christmas to my Mom, love and kisses, Robert.

At my message shows I am guided by spirit to buy presents and this one time I had to buy a potted plant. It was for the Mum of someone in the audience. It was from her first husband who had passed. I tried to fight with him and say get something nicer but he was adamant that this plant was the one he wanted. It was a purple colour but very basic. The daughter took the plant to give to her Mum, not understanding it fully because her Mum and Dad had not been together at the time he passed. He wanted her to know he still had feelings for her and was around. Later the daughter had confirmed that the plant her Dad had bought for her Mum had been the exact same one he had bought for her when she was born! He wanted the Mum to remember the special moments.

One day when Carol was cleaning out a box of her father-in-laws things, helping his wife through the hard task of getting rid of some of his old papers, he left a gift for her, it was a medallion and on it were a rainbow and a dove. The Rainbow was Carol's Mums sign to her and the Dove was her Dads sign to her. Carol indeed felt a huge blessing knowing that they were altogether on the other side helping each other and helping them. What a true gift!

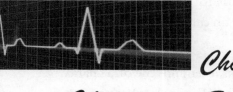

Chapter 27
Christmas Spirit

The week before my Christmas with Heaven show I was awakened by a young girl in spirit called Grace. I was aware she had a younger brother here on earth. Grace was bouncing around showing me that she gets her brother excited with her excitement! It was 3:30 in the morning, I could hear the jingle bells ringing; Grace was showing me the magic of Christmas. I felt like a kid again.

Grace is a fun little girl and can plant thoughts into her brothers head so he does things he can get in trouble for. If she was living on earth her brother would have gotten into trouble for all kinds of things she would have instigated. Grace sees a present under the Christmas tree for herself. She takes it and gives it to a sick child in hospital who otherwise would have nothing, the girl in hospital is about seven or eight years old, very skinny laying in a bed, tubes hooked up to her. She is lonely because no one is there with her – she has leukaemia.

Many times before doing a show I can have spirits come to me during the week for me to pass messages on to their loved ones here on earth during the show.

Graces parents confirmed they place a gift for their daughter under the tree every Christmas to keep her memory alive for themselves and her brother. Grace has a spirit that is full of generosity, fun and love. Because Grace's parents honour her every Christmas and every birthday they allow Grace's spirit to grow to the age she would have been if she had been living on earth. Grace grows with her family.

I personally would like to thank Grace as it reminds me of a charity I headed up in Canada called The Tree of Angels where people would buy gifts for children who had nothing. This is something I need to look into doing in England, or for the sick children in the hospital who really have nothing except disease. As this book heads to publication this year's Christmas with Heaven show charity proceeds are going towards Bristol's children hospital. I am doing mini readings to help out Bodmin College Beauty year three girls for their fundraiser for terminal ill children at Treliske Hospital here in Cornwall, England. I feel passionate about helping these worthwhile charities.

To all of you I hope this Christmas you can spread a little joy to someone in need. Feel the gentle grace of this little girl; feel it in your heart ; feel the sparkle and magic of Grace; feel all the love, take some of it and spread it and spread it some more. You will make a huge difference, even though it might not seem like a lot to you, it will mean a lot to someone else. So go on spread love, and spread some more – go beyond Christmas and start doing it every day all year through.

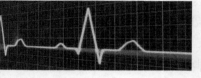

Chapter 28
Trusting Spirit

I n doing this journey something you learn along the way is to TRUST, trust that spirit can see the higher (bigger) picture! – Easier said than done sometimes.

At the beginning when I started getting messages for people I would shake inside as I resisted giving the messages. I would argue with spirit saying no what if it was wrong? What if they did not get it? But the shaking would not stop until I gave the message.

One day as I was working in my day job at the bank, a man entered who looked about mid fifty's to sixty's. I had never seen him before but I instantly felt his wife with him. Now I tried very hard to keep my bank job separate from my psychic work but this day spirit had other plans. The man's wife was telling me to tell him that she was with him but I refused and said no. What if he does not believe? He may complain and I would get into trouble at work. She was persistent and I began to shake inside. The man went into an office with a loans officer and I told his wife if he was alone then I would give the message. At that moment the loans officer got up and left the office – he was now indeed alone! So I took the chance and went in and told him what I did and his wife wanted to say hello. She told him she knew their daughter was getting married and she could see blue bridesmaid's dresses. She also described a church with three stained glass windows in it. She told her husband to tell their daughter that she would be at the wedding and her daughter should not be sad that her Mom would not be there. It would be a beautiful day. The man said "a year ago before my wife died I would not have believed this but too much has happened since she has gone. It is true my daughter is getting married and her bridesmaid dresses are blue, the church you are describing was the church my wife had her funeral in so my daughter will be getting married outside. My daughter will be happy to know it will be a nice day and that her Mom will be there for her. Thank you so much you are indeed an angel."

After that my shaking stopped and the man left and I never saw him again. I was so glad I trusted spirit to relay such an important message.

After years of this I knew enough to trust spirit. A few years ago I was guided to come back to England to be with Steve who was my first boyfriend at the age of thirteen. When we met up again over thirty years later it was like being hit by thunder and lightning! We knew something was happening to us as we both felt like we were being pulled into a tunnel of energy, the force too strong for us to handle. I tried to fight it, after all my life was in Canada with my family, but I could not; I knew on a higher level that I had a purpose with Steve and back in England. We both knew at some point we would get married we knew each other inside out on a deeper level without knowing how!

On a return visit to Canada Jeneen had come from Saskatchewan to visit me in Manitoba for a few days to do some classes with me. Jeneen said that your Uncle Mike is with you – Mike's sign to me are ladybugs/ladybirds and we were seeing them everywhere. A couple of days later Jeneen and myself decided to treat ourselves and go to a hotel so we could do some energy work on each other and the following day we were going shopping. Jeneen herself has great awareness when it comes to following energy. She has a deep knowing and I would always trust her. We usually went to a particular shopping mall but this time she wanted to go to another one I was like yes that is fine. As we were walking in the mall a lady handed me a brochure, we looked and it was for a jewellery store. Jeneen said" let's go in and see what kind of engagement rings look good on you." We did but I did not find anything I liked or wanted. We went for a coffee in the centre of the mall and when I looked at the name of the store it was called "Michael Hill". I was floored because that was Mike's name! It was like he was guiding me to try on rings. Then Jeneen saw another jewellery store opposite and said lets go in there so we did. I tried on a ring and loved it. It was the perfect ring as I love sparkle and that is what it did! I decided to buy it knowing I would propose to Steve when I got back to England. I no longer do things the traditional way! Jeneen said she was going to the clothing store next door and for me to meet her there. When I went in the song that was playing in the store was "Will you marry me?" We just looked at each other and said validation, proof I had done the right thing! Thank you to Mike for guiding me and being there for me, giving me fun when I get too serious. I love you Mike, you are and always will be my second Dad xo

When we don't go with what is for our highest good we will become unhappy inside, even discontented as we are trying to live through what others want for us, knowing it is not always best for our souls growth.

Chapter 29
Where are They?

While doing a reading for an older woman Doris her husband Joe came through. I remember it being a cold winter's day in Canada with lots of snow. Joe was so concerned for his wife he could see her going to the cemetery every day and getting cold. He wanted her to stay warm. He was at home with her in their house. Joe was with her all the time. He showed that she took the bible out and read a passage every evening before going to sleep and he could hear her saying goodnight to him. This couple had been married for over fifty five years and there was obviously so much love between them. Doris felt better, knowing his concern for her so when it was storming or too cold she would not go to the cemetery. She would only go on the days when it was warmer. Joe knew how much his wife loved and missed him and wanted to continue the commitment they had to each other by going to the cemetery every day. Doris understood now that she was still committed to Joe every day whether she went to the cemetery or not.

Please know that if you are that person that feels the need to visit the cemetery everyday to keep your loved one close to you; then go – the choice will always be yours but please do not feel guilty if there is a day that you cannot make it for whatever reason. Your loved one will be with you wherever you go; they are always in your heart. Many of them follow you to the cemetery and kneel with you. They put their arm around you as they see your tears flow. For some people it makes them feel better to place flowers on a grave or to make sure it looks nice. It is a way of being able to make a difference. This is your journey and you must do it your way.

Our loved ones are all around us. Some just come for a visit and some can split themselves in multiple ways and be with more than one family member at a time. At one of my recent shows I had a Mum come through for her son saying she splits herself at least twenty ways between her children and grandchildren. He validated this would be true as there was over twenty of them! His Mum had lived for her children and grandchildren.

From my experience I feel that everyone has some one with them at all times. These can be loved ones, spirit guides, animal guides, angels, archangels, teachers and even spirits from past lives. Whatever you are going through in life please know that you are never alone and you can call upon anyone of these at any time.

Chapter 30
On Top of the World

I had reconnected with an old school friend through Face book. Bonnie was someone that I had gone to school with when I first immigrated to Canada at the age of fifteen. Bonnie was that fun girl who had the brightest smile and the cutest dimples. Bonnie's whole family were really nice or at least the ones I met. When I would go to Bonnie's house it was "come on in, the more the merrier". I remember having a few good parties at Bonnie's house – it was always a fun time.

Through the years we lost contact but I connected with her sister Lorie and her family through the bank where I worked. One day I was looking for a venue to do one of my message evenings when Lorie suggested I do it where she worked. Lorie arranged this for me and she came to the message evening and told Bonnie about it. Bonnie contacted me via Face book and we started to chat a little.

Bonnie was interested herself in having a session with me. We set up a time but she had to cancel due to something that had come up. We set up another time but again Bonnie had to cancel; it was as if somehow Bonnie was scared of what I was going to say. I told Bonnie her Dad was with her and would help her but she was afraid he would be upset with her. I reassured her that he was not. She seemed a little easier and set up another appointment. However it was not meant to be because Bonnie died suddenly of a Brain aneurysm, she was the young age of fifty two. I was having a message evening in Canada soon after and Bonnie's sister Lorie arrived with Bonnie's daughter Miranda and some other family members. Bonnie came through for her family but had wanted them to have a private ceremony with some of the other family members. I felt Bonnie's energy was lower, she had crossed over but there was still a cloud of judgement around her —Bonnie did not feel enough of herself – which was stopping her from going higher. Bonnie gave gifts to some of her family there that night.

Lorie set up a date for me to come to her house. She had no idea that I needed to help Bonnie to go to a higher level on the other side. Bonnie did not want me to tell her. I had to tell Lorie to pick out two pieces of music that reminded her of Bonnie. Bonnie asked me to take a gift for every person who was attending that day. I had to give everyone a playing card and rip it in half and put the other half in a bowl. I had to take two beautiful ceramic doves, one had a stretched out wing over the other dove for protection. I had to place them in the centre of the table with a lit candle to honour Bonnie. I felt so strongly that Bonnie's daughter Miranda should get the doves but I left it to fate and the spirits. I asked Lorie to play the first song which was "Hello" by Adele "Hello from the outside, I'm sorry for breaking your heart... Hello from the other side" seemed very appropriate for today. Everyone lit a candle and one by one everyone said what Bonnie was to them – how she had made a difference in their lives. As each person said something I could see the cloud falling away from Bonnie, she never realized what a contribution she had made. As the last person said how she felt, it was as if Bonnie became free, she went to a higher level. I drew the cards for the ceramic doves and her daughter Miranda won them. I told Miranda her Mom would always protect her and if she was thinking of getting a tattoo to look at the wings. I continued to draw cards for the gifts and with each one there was a message, a personalized message from Bonnie. Her sister Lorie received a bracelet called "freedom" with a bird on it; she had received the same one the night of the message evening from Bonnie so there are no coincidences, a double message! I thanked everyone for being so wonderful, for all the strong love and for helping Bonnie go to a higher level. Amongst this group were wonderful family members as well as long-time best friends. I told Lorie can you play the next song now. The song was "on top of the world" by The Carpenters. I find it fascinating how appropriate the songs were seeing Lorie had no idea we were taking Bonnie to a new level and I had no idea what songs Lorie had picked out. It was the work of Bonnie and her way of saying Thank you! "I am now on top of the world looking down on creation".

Bonnie continues to give messages. As soon as I was finished at Lorie's I had another reading to do and when I got there Chris's daughter Juliette was colouring me a picture. After I had finished doing her Dad's reading she gave me the picture and said "this is for you". It was a rainbow bird and I knew it was for Miranda. I asked Juliette if I could give this to a girl who's Mommy had gone to heaven and she said "yes rainbow kisses from her Mommy". When I got home I messaged Miranda to say she should have rainbow wings and she said she had just finished saying she was thinking of having rainbow wings tattooed! It was a validation from her Mom. Upon my return to England one night while sleeping Bonnie woke me up and I knew I had to message Miranda. I told her that her Mom knew she was having a hard time especially seeing this would be her first Christmas without her. Bonnie showed me angel wings on the tree. I told Miranda this and she confirmed that she had just decorated the tree and instead of the star they usually put on top she had put an angel on it with beautiful angel wings. It was Bonnie's way of saying to Miranda I was there with you! Another time when Bonnie woke me up (she likes the night time) she gave Miranda a butterfly. I told her one would come to her attention, she would really notice it. Miranda told me she was just drinking out of a cup that had a butterfly on it! While typing this chapter it is Valentine's Day and Bonnie wanted me to message Miranda to say thank you, thank you for the single flower. Miranda said weird, my boyfriend gave me a bunch of flowers today and while I picked them up one broke off, usually I would have thrown it away but we picked it up and put it in a glass. This was Bonnie's way of saying "I am here, Happy Valentine's Day, I love you!"

"I'm on top of the world looking down on creation and the only explanation I can find is the love that I've found ever since you've been around your love's put me at the top of the world!"

Chapter 31
The Loneliness of Death

After the death of your spouse, the one you have been with for years, the one you gave your right arm for, the one who is your constant companion, your best friend, the one who knew you better than anyone -when they are gone – the funeral and shock over with – when everyone else goes back to their normal lives – there is just you; just you and the black hole of loneliness. The loneliness of trying to cope without your loved one here on earth. You feel so very lost. It is easier during the day when it is daylight and people are around and you can be out and about. It is when the darkness comes, when you have to draw the curtains, when you are inside all alone. The loneliness that you feel so deep inside and you just want them back. Back to talk to, to make a cup of tea for. The TV can only be a companion for so long. You try and avoid it but you must go to bed and pull back the covers and get into a cold bed – a reminder that they are no longer with you and not coming back. The tears that fall are silent, no one can hear them, and no one knows how much your heart is breaking; how much you are missing them, how much you long to be with them once more.

This is how a teenager felt when she lost her Mom. I just want my Mom; she is the one who was always there for me no matter what. She loved me so much and now she is gone! Who is going to guide me when I get married? Who is going to help me when I have my first child? I get angry at my friends when they complain about their Moms. Do they know how lucky they are just to have a Mom? I wish my Mom was here. I feel so all alone there is no one to pick up the pieces anymore – just me – I have to cope with it all; with all these hidden feelings tucked away inside. When I try to be strong for my other family members – when all I want to do is shrivel up and die so I can be with my Mom again. I want to get a message from my Mom. Where is she? Why did she have to leave me so young? Oh what I would do to feel those loving arms around me once more telling me that everything is going to be alright. It is not ok Mom; I miss you more with each passing day. People say it gets easier but I have not seen that yet. No one understands how hard this is – they cannot see the ache inside my heart. If they could listen to my heart they would be able to hear it screaming. Help me someone, when will this loneliness go away?

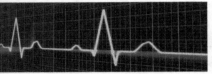

Chapter 32
Party Time

Everyone was yelling come to the party! Come on let's have a few more drinks at the house party! Hesitantly she went, thinking she should go home but she was having so much fun! The night continued – what a blast she was having with these amazing friends.

As the party was winding down they realized everyone had too much to drink – she said she would drive but her friend said she was too drunk and should not drive! A younger male said he would drive them home they did not live far away. He seemed ok so they got in the car and he started driving fast, he continued to go faster and faster, showing off because he liked one of the girls. They told him to slow down but he lost control of the car and slammed into a tree. One was dead and the other two were ambulanced to hospital.

The friend lived, she felt guilty why did she encourage her friend to come to the party? Why had they got in that car? How will the driver live with himself knowing that he killed someone? Everyone is mad with them!

The realization was that it was her time to go. She had taught all of her lessons on earth; no one was listening to her anymore. Now she could teach more in death and from the other side. Many lessons will be learnt. Her friend who felt guilty had to see it from a different perspective.

The driver had shouldered the blame; he was willing to be so strong and accepted being charged for her death. He and her friend saved her from her being the one driving and dying as a drunk driver because her family could not have coped with that. This way she died with dignity, for the beautiful fun loving person she was.

It has not even been a day and she is on the other side communicating. She has a dog and her grandmother with her. She is picking a single daisy for her Mom and throwing it down to her. Her Mom is blinded by all the emotion so she can't see it yet. "Mom I know you will miss me every single day – thank you for being the one to sit with me and hold me in my darkest times. Now it's my turn to sit and hold you in your darkest hour."

Mom,

Please do not be mad or upset with anyone. It was nearly me that drove that car drunk and my friend saved me. She saved me and you from that torture.

Mom you were the one that was always there for me. You tried to help me many a time but I did not listen, I had to do it my way. I get it now, I get that you loved me no matter what. Look up Mom I am in the stars that shine brightly and I will always be looking down on you. I am freeeeeeeeeeeee! It is a wonderful feeling to feel so light.

— (the dash has yet to be written)

Keep playing your music Mom, I will always love you xo

Yes it is true that I am not coming back in this physical body again but I am coming back in my spirit. I will come back many a time to be with you. Feel me all around you as I kiss you goodnight!

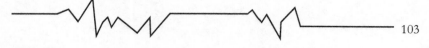

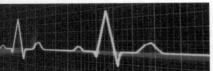

Chapter 33
One Step at a Time

Slowly as if time has almost stopped; you have a thick fog around you, you feel very lethargic, every muscle heavy like lead; how do you move forward?

The ache in your heart when you can't see their smiling face anymore, or even their frown – oh how you long to feel their arms around you once more; what you wouldn't do to laugh with them or to even argue with them once more.

Then panic sets in; what if you can't remember anymore? What if you can't remember what it was like to hold them? What if you can't remember their laugh? Or how their skin felt? What if you forget them? Your head is screaming; PLEASE COME BACK! Take me back in time! How do I reverse this?

A new day begins it is so hard to put that foot outside of that bed but somehow you do; you have to as there are others that need you; even though you don't care – you just want to scream and cry your heart out because it hurts so much; how can you go on?

One foot in front of the other, that is about all you can handle for now. People are speaking to you but it sounds like a foreign language only garbled. It is strange your brain is too foggy and just does not comprehend anything.

I want my child back; please bring them back to me!

Wow! What did I ever do to deserve this? What could I have done differently? I wish my head would stop screaming; I'm so tired; it is too much work to put that foot in front of the other. I just need to lie down and fall asleep. My mind is too foggy and the chatter is too loud, I can't fall asleep, it is too hard to function.

Help me please how do I get out of this? Oh I know one foot in front of the other. I have to try after all I have other people here who love me, but some days it is hard to find the energy to care. I will try to put one lead foot in front of the other. Time is so slow; everyone tells me it will heal, the pain will subside; but I don't feel any different I lost a piece of me and I can't get it back; so now I have to learn to live with life all over again in a very different way.

One day I woke up and my feet moved a little easier. I could breathe a little better and I could see through the fog a little clearer; the ache in my heart was beginning to just be something that felt normal to me – still there but not foreign anymore.

Too many people were around me before and now there are not enough; are they forgetting my child already? How can they? How dare they? Oh how I long to see my child again, to hold them in my arms and tell them how much I love them; did they really know how much I loved them? The world has changed for me forever; why is everything so different now?

It has been a while now and people mean well but I just want to scream at them "you just don't understand!" How do I get my child back? Even though I can take one step in front of the other because I am used to it now; some days it is still hard to breathe.

One day I noticed the sun was shining. I did not think I had seen it for a while. I don't remember any more. I felt a little warm; I don't think I remember that feeling either as I have been numb for so long.

On that day someone had told me we are all energy and my child had just changed form; how could that be? They explained it is like water to steam. They told me to place my hand on my heart and feel their love; I closed my eyes and for a split second could see my child standing and smiling at me. I could feel their love in my heart; it seemed so real they were and always would be in my heart. My step seemed lighter that day; maybe this is possible after all.

I was told that my child was around me even though I could not physically see them; when we allow ourselves to feel, we can feel them, maybe our hair moves or it's a whispers touch on your cheek. I do believe I can feel them; maybe even in a tickle. I was told they bring lots of things to us when we allow ourselves to open up and see. They bring sunshine to us in all ways and special little signs like birds or butterflies, flowers, animals, rainbows, feathers and all kinds of special messages. They always have a special sign to you if you can look and see. I can hear them in their whispers and the calling of my name, sometimes even when I hear a song on the radio I feel they are speaking to me. Yes I do believe they are around me, in the air that I breathe and the wind that caresses my soul.

My heart still cries to see the real thing but if I close my eyes for just a moment, it is like they are here in my heart, smiling and loving me.

They pick my feet up, maybe I can go on. I need to open up all my senses again; sometimes I can smell them and hear their laughter; the more I am aware of all my senses the more ways they can come to me.

I thank you my darling child for helping me to see so differently. You bought me the greatest joy and happiness along with the deepest despair of sorrow. How can I go on? I can knowing you are in my heart and soul and every inch of me. I can go on knowing you are helping to put the spring back in my step; allowing me to put one step in front of the other.

Thank you for teaching me so much. I will forever love you and hold you in my heart.

Chapter 34
Spirits from Past Lives

I t is not always spirits that come through from this life time for people. You can have ancestors from this life time that you knew and often ancestors that you have never even met. Some can have spirit guides, teachers and souls from past lives.

When I was giving a reading to Nora a little boy came through for her. He was around the age of two with blonde hair, a chubby happy little boy. I knew he belonged to the present and would be coming into her life one day in this life time. Nora also had two young girls with her who looked like they were around five and six, they were very dark haired and skinny; they looked identical except one was a little taller; they looked like spitting images of their Mummy. I could see these daughters were from a past life she had in Spain and I could see a fire burning in which her daughters perished and died. I told her that I felt in her subconscious mind that part of her did not want children in this life time because she was afraid of losing them and did not want to go through the death of a child. It would be too much for her soul to bear. Wow she was amazed as she had never told anyone but opened up to me that she felt she had a son even though she had no physical children in this world. She also had a great fear of fire in this life time and admitted she and her husband had been trying for a baby for two years. Somewhere inside she knew there was nothing physically wrong with her and that she had the awareness of a "blockage" even though she was not sure what it was. After a few sessions of emotional releasing and removing the energy block inside of her Nora was indeed able to get pregnant.

When doing a reading for Marianne I could see a little girl around her. She was a very happy little girl even though I could see she had a disability of one leg shorter than the other. This little girl had polio when she was a baby. I could see her living in the country playing around a big tree. This tree had a swing for her to use and enjoy and she spent many hours alone with the tree. I could see that her parents were very over protective of her. They did not want the other children to tease her so thought they were doing the best thing by not allowing her to play with others. They kept her home by herself. They did not want her to go through the pain and suffering that comes from teasing. I told Marianne that there was a "protection issue" around her as she was still carrying this in her energy. She had been this little girl in a past life. Marianne confirmed that in this life time she was also an only child and her parents had also been overly protective of her. Marianne was trying not to do the same to her children but found it very difficult at times. After this session she was able to let go of the need to protect.

Past lives can have such an impact on us because we are the same soul in a different body in a different time and we carry information in our cell memory. This is why emotions and information need to be released at the cell memory level so you will not have to carry that forward into another life time.

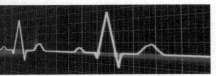

Chapter 35
Lesson Learnt

While doing a reading for Ed a past life came up for him. Ed and his third wife in this life time Sharon had been married to each other in a previous lifetime where he had lived in London, England and had been a "Bobby" policeman. They had five children in the order of boy girl boy girl boy. They were married for fifty six wonderful years. Their fourth child a girl had been very sick with scarlet fever, she reincarnated into this life time as Sharon's grandmother who had also had scarlet fever when she was younger. Sharon had a son who passed away ten days after Ed and Sharon got married. He came through in the reading and told Ed that he had learnt the lesson of being his son and no longer needed to be here; he had been one of their sons in their previous married life time. He was happy for them and would guide them on the rest of their journey together here on earth.

Ed and Sharon said it made total sense because after their previous spouses died, Ed and Sharon had lived next door to each other and felt they knew each other before they actually did. They were on the same page and felt totally content and connected with each other.

Ed was also told he would not be coming back to earth anymore. He was going to be a guide and with that he changed into a man with long white hair in a ponytail, with a long white beard. He wore a white gown and carried a gold staff. I had a deep knowing that Ed would show himself to me after his death and help me with a piece I will need to learn so I can help take myself and others to a new level.

Ed told me it made sense because even in this life time he had overcome addictions of alcoholism and smoking. He had lost two wives to illness as well as a son and a grandson. He was learning so much spiritually such as forgiveness because he had to forgive himself for how he treated his family when he was an alcoholic. He forgave himself for abusing his body and avoiding his soul. Ed has taken meditation classes and connected to his inner self, he has totally found peace with himself and all his earthly lives. Ed has done much of this in his seventy's so when someone says "I am too old!" think again – maybe it is time to let go and heal so you don't take it with you on your next journey.

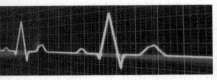

Chapter 36

A Skeptic

I had received a message from Angela asking if I would do her a phone reading; she had let me know she was quite skeptical as she had received some great readings and some bad fake readings in the past.

When I tuned into Angela I could see a dark green aura and knew instantly this was about letting go of family and their beliefs as they were not a fit to her energy field. I saw at least ten family members in spirit from her Father's side of the family. One lady stood out and I knew this was a Great Great Great Grandmother for her, she was dressed in a long dress with a white half apron; she was thinly built with thin brown hair. This Great Great Great grandmother energy was moving like a zombie, very robotically. The Great Great Great grandmother showed me she had lost a son who was only a few days old, she was still grieving him as she had not been allowed to grieve while she lived here on Earth because she had to look after her husband and assist with the chores and the other children; her heart ached for her son. He had died of lack of oxygen and blood issues. After the death of her son she had only existed; I knew she was a ghost as she was so zombie looking to me.

At first I could tell that Angela did not want to hear about the members of her Father's family. I was going to move on to the tarot card reading but she said that is not what she wanted she had wanted to hear from someone specific. When I tuned back into the spirits the Great Great Great grandmothers energy came forth again and said that Angela herself was carrying her vibration of loss and suffering. Angela admitted she herself had lost a son in this life time at only a few days old with the exact same symptoms as her Great Great Great grandmother's son. I told her she was the chosen one to break the cycle of this family loss; she was chosen to heal the Great Great Great Grandmother's energy. We cleared the Great Great Great Grandmothers spirit so she could go into a lighter vibrational state. She immediately thanked Angela and said to her she was having issues with her own family as she was very different. Angela's purpose was to bring peace to the world and to work with clearing ghost like energies – those caught between the worlds so they could be at peace again. Angela could also help people in this world who had lost babies – as she would have compassion and understanding for what they had gone through.

Angela asked me to tune into her baby that had died. I told her that I could feel his love and could see his soul had reincarnated into her second son living here on earth. Her deceased son's purpose was to help heal the Great Great Great Grandmothers energy as his soul had also been her son who had died – he had now come back to earth into Angela's second son. This time he would live a full healthy life on earth. Angela confirmed she and her husband had a suspicion that her son who had died was her second sons' energy as they looked alike.

Angela was absolutely amazed as all this resonated with her. I helped her do some emotional releasing – releasing grief, sadness and loss. Angela said this is what she had been searching for as she had always felt this deep inside of her. She told me I had cracked the code for her; changing her life and course in a positive way. She told me this was the most different reading she had ever had as I could see her soul purpose.

– Angela: no longer a skeptic.

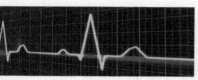

Chapter 37
Karma from Past Lives

(Karma – the total effect of a person's actions and conduct during the successive phases of his existence, regarded as determining his next incarnation)

Julie had been asking spirit for an answer to a specific question: "should I continue to take some spousal support money from my husband?" She shouted at spirit to give her a sign as this was causing her some grief in her divorce with some family members especially one of her daughters. A lady in spirit appeared before her and she showed Julie a vision of one of her past lives.

Julie could see a big old Victorian style house in England. An older lady who had fine white hair neatly placed in a bun on the top of her head showed her to a room. She told Julie "this is where you will be staying." The room had a four poster bed with a fireplace; a small table with an old fashioned jug and wash basin. The floorboards were bare and wooden. Julie was very pregnant with a heavy long navy blue dress on – she was about twenty one which was old in those days. An older man (James her husband in this life time) around thirty six had told Julie he loved her and if she had sex with him he would leave his wife and marry her. Julie thought

"I'm old – no one else will want me, I am a virgin and I have never been treated the way he treats me. He showers me with gifts and kindness." Julie had sex with him and when she got pregnant he told her he could not leave his wife he still loved her and they would raise the baby. Julie wanted the baby.

In the boarding house Julie had to sit on a long wooden table with nine others. Beside her sat a very young girl about sixteen. It was Barb (her best friend in this life time) she had brought shame to her family. Julie became very protective over her and she became the "little sister" she never had.

Julie gave birth to a little girl (Sophie, her oldest daughter in this life time). Julie loved her daughter and wanted to raise her by herself but she was told she couldn't because she had no money and no job. The father and his wife took her daughter. That was their plan all along because the wife could not have children. Julie's daughter grew up as an only child. A few years later Julie made her way to Scotland going to their mansion; this was no easy trek as most of it was on foot. Julie did not care as she longed to get a glimpse of her daughter. There had not been a day when she had not thought of her. Julie stood outside in the cold; she looked in the window through the wrought iron bars that surrounded the property and saw Sophie who was about four. It was Christmas time and there was a brightly burning fire and a beautiful big tree. Sophie had ringlets in her hair and she was playing with a lovely doll house.

Julie thought she is growing up not knowing the truth; not knowing her real Mom loves her so very much.

James is paying his karmic debt back and that is why Julie needed to take some spousal support money. (James and Julie are helping each other with this; as they agreed upon this lesson before they came to earth.) James took everything from Julie once, including her daughter and it is his choice because he can take her again, but then he won't be learning his lesson and will have to come back to earth again. It is interesting because even in this life time James wowed Julie with expensive gifts at the beginning of their relationship; Julie was going to break up with him but did not want to give his gold bracelet back as no one had ever given her such an expensive piece of jewellery!

Julie now understood she had kept this in her cell memory, as she could not understand it as she was not normally a materialistic person.

Julie did not fully understand Karma before she was shown this piece. She always thought what you put out in this life time will come back now, she now understands that we can be paying our debts back from previous life times and also in turn it can take another life time for you to be paid back for all the good you have done.

It is indeed hard to understand everything; many things stay in our cell memory. When Julie told Barb about this vision she said it made sense to her because in this life time she was adamant that she could not get pregnant before she was eighteen, it scared her so much that she choose the only way that was 100% fool proof — she chose to abstain from sex somewhere knowing she was fertile, knowing she did not want to bring shame to her family. She did not know why she felt so strongly about that when she was younger but now it made sense to her."

Please be careful what you choose I know someone who chose to swindle his brother out of his inheritance from his mother. He lied and cheated on his own mother when he was in charge of her affairs, (power of attorney) saying "sign here you are getting new windows," when all the time his intention was to take a second mortgage on her house so he could have the money for himself. When his mother died he told his brother who lived in another country he would forward him his share of the money. He promised his brother he would send him the money time and time again and it never arrived. In the end the brother who had cheated everyone out of their money ended up bankrupt. He chose money over family. Then a few years later he found his own son dead on Christmas day at the age of forty. The universe said you chose money over family so we are taking your family from you.

Be careful what are you choosing. Are you treating people the way you would like to be treated? Do not worry about what others are doing, instead focus on what you are doing. Remember how people treat you is their Karma; what you do and how you react is yours. Life will give you whatever experiences are most helpful for the evolution of your consciousness.

Lesson of time – Karma

Time and circumstances can change at any time. Don't devalue or hurt anyone in life. You may be powerful today. But remember. Time is more powerful than you! One tree makes a million match sticks... only one match stick is needed to burn a million trees... so be good and do good.

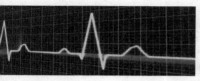

Chapter 38
All Levels

I used to believe that spirit all came from one place – all above from a place called "Heaven". They were all kind loving souls, our ancestors whom we loved and they loved us and they were meant to guide us. I now understand that is not so. There are many other levels on the other side. There are good, bad and ugly spirits on the other side just like there are here on earth. As at the beginning of this book when I had the experience of the spirits who I thought were going to kill me – they were some of the lower energies, they did not come from the level of love. For me I did not want to see that horrible scary energy, I was not ready to see that. I wanted to choose to only see love, to see all the good things; so, I refused to see anything but good. I chose to look at the good in every single person but now I realize you need to see the bad and ugly also as it can be a great healing tool. You need to see the truth if only for your knowledge and goodness. There is no judgement in the truth. If one of your so called friends turned out to be a paedophile you would need to know for your information so you could keep your children out of reach from them. Most paedophiles seem like "nice" people. They are very good at fooling people and hiding who they really are from the world.

During my journey back to England I looked deep inside of myself. I did some great healing work on a deep level. In doing so I was able to see deeper, to see beyond my previous limits. I could see the good, bad and ugly. I became aware that there was so much more. I became aware that as my light shone brighter the dark energies wanted to put me out. I knew when the dark tried to enter into my vibration. I was no longer afraid of anything I was shown. I was aware that when I needed to work with someone who had a lot of negativity around them I would get sick as the dark energies did not want me to clear them of any lower energy. I am not afraid as I know I am stronger than they are! The darkness is only fear and separation. I believe we all came from the light at one point in creation; as we descended down to Earth (which is a lower frequency) we forgot and we became separated from the true light. You can conquer anything when you connect to your being – your soul – your light. The light is always stronger than the dark. When you shine light onto dark; the dark will disappear.

When I worked on my client Michelle her dad came through for her and I said you might not like what I have to say but I have to be honest. Your Dad has a lot of evil energy around him and he is coming up from the underground – a very low level. Michelle was like Thank you! You are the first medium to ever say that. My Dad was an evil man and I always felt he was at a different level. Between Michelle and me we were able to clear his demons and lower energies so he could go to a higher frequency. Michelle was not able to forgive her dad totally at that time so we converted her dad into an energy ball which she was able to forgive and send higher so if need be she could draw on energy from the energy ball. So yes there are indeed demon like energies and god like energies and everything in between. I am sure I have not seen it all yet but I am open to receiving every energy as I evolve and understand the spirit realms even more.

John came to see me for a reading; as soon as he came in I knew he was different to most people on earth as his aura and energy was so bright. John's Mum came through for him and she told him that she would not be coming back to earth anymore. She was very much entwined with John's energy. He admitted he had a hard time moving forward since his Mum passed a year before as she was his business partner and they were very close. His Mum told John that he also would not be coming back to Earth after this life time. I could see a very wise spirit with him and told John he would be a master guide and working on that level. He should not wait and start being that master guide on earth right now. He has the ability to teach what he knows. He said this made sense as he had a dream years before that he was sat around a table with twelve men and they said "someone has to go back to earth to learn" – it was him. I told him he had to learn all about the feminine side of things. Again this made sense as in this life time John was gay; he was also very creative as he was an artist. We need both female and male energies to be balanced. John had to learn more about the feminine aspect of life; John would be returning to the level of the master guides when he has learnt the piece required for the afterlife. His Mum was working to bring truth and integrity to earth, something she had learned in the life she had just finished. This was part of her soul purpose. I asked John if he happened to die before me if he would come find me and give me information so I can help more people with the higher purpose here on earth.

While doing some energy work with Emma her master guide came through for her. He was in an old library surrounded by knowledgeable books; he looked like someone who would appear on Lord of the Rings or Dumbledore from Harry Potter. If Emma needed to know anything she had to ask him and he would give her the knowledge required. He said his name was "Siri". Afterwards it came to our attention that was the same name when you ask questions to an iPhone. Interesting – I believe information is down loaded to us and this was a confirmation for Emma. (If you

Google "Siri" it does say it is "an intelligent personal assistant from Apple".) I had also given someone a message to let her know her son had transitioned to the level of the wise men; he was in the library of knowledge – he loved to read and was a very wise man. He had learnt his piece down here on Earth and took it back to the library. He was now sharing more knowledge with the world by implanting educational thoughts into people's minds.

The moment Martin stepped through the door he said "what is the purpose of life – what's my purpose?" I replied "I'm seeing you converting old decrepit buildings and turning them into something beautiful. That is what you have to learn here on earth to help you with your soul's purpose. Your soul's purpose is to help repair the damaged ugly souls on earth and turn them into beauty again." Martin confirmed he had just bought a big old building which would take about five years to restore. You see Martin had to learn this in the physical – he had to pass this test here on earth to be qualified to work on the higher levels when he dies.

At one of my shows Marie's daughter came through to say "everything that is happening to you on Earth is for you to learn patience. You are having trouble with your son because of drugs – which involves lies. You are keeping calm, learning the patience of a saint because when you die you will be working on the level with the saints." Many people can have some level of patience but "the patience of a saint" is the highest level you can achieve. Marie had been thrown test after test here on Earth; this will be Marie's last earthly incarnation as she will transition into the saintly realm.

In Mary's reading a young male called Doug came through who had taken his life; he was caught between the levels so we transitioned him to the other side with love and light. As we did this I saw a male energy with a long grey beard holding a lantern being a bright light so Doug could see the way. Mary's soul's purpose was to be that light for lost souls when she went to the other side.

Mary's life had been full of abuse especially verbal abuse. Her lesson was to keep her light shining here on earth; this takes great inner strength and only the strongest of souls can do this. It is so important when working on that level on the other side to keep that light bright. It is like the lighthouse here on earth which saved many a ship by keeping their light shining bright. Many humans allow others to dim their light. Most humans take things too personally as they cannot see the bigger picture. Nothing is as it seems here on earth when you start to look beyond. Mary needed those abusive people in her life so she could learn to keep her energy high; her light shining – she had to learn to never let anyone dull her sparkle; this was all a part of her test. Mary had the choice she could pass the test this life time or she can come back and do it in another life time.

For Mark his soul's purpose was to contain any viruses. In this life time he had recently been diagnosed with Parkinson's disease. Since being "sick" he had become aware of who was talking about him behind his back and who his true friends were. He had to learn who he could trust. He was learning to sense the dark energies and the light energies. I could see Mark would be working in a lab on the other side on a spaceship – his job would be to contain all the viruses so the galaxies and universes would not get contaminated; he needed to know that all who worked in his lab would be trustworthy. I could see a man at Marks work that was helping him with his journey on earth. He would be his assistant in the lab; this man was his assistant here on earth as they had to learn how to work together. Marks wife would also be working on the spaceship and she herself had to learn how to enjoy the sanctuary of their home as she would have to learn to live in the spaceship.

I believe there are hundreds of levels on the other side – we all have a soul's purpose. The first level is a heavier level – the highest level is pure light. For me from what I have been shown so far I am from the love source energy – learning unconditional love and acceptance. To do this I need people in my life who don't accept me and my actions; so I can still accept and love them. We live in a dual world so I need people who love me unconditionally and people who love me conditionally so I can learn the difference. I am grateful for the couple of people who love me so much on a higher level that they chose to help me with this lesson. They can't see it as they do not remember what we agreed on before we came to earth – they will when we are all in the light again. I have chosen to learn this lesson so I will be able to work with all levels on the other side. I am willing to go to any level embracing everyone with love so I can make a positive difference. Part of my test is to keep believing in me no matter what anyone says; this takes great inner strength.

I have met two people on earth who are from the pure light. One is Lena; a child born with complications. Lena is unable to talk yet and I believe she will not do so in this life time. Lena is from the highest level so if she talks she will become tainted – remember words and love get tainted – pure light cannot. She has come to teach her parents and family how to telepathically communicate with her; I know her Dad Chris is learning to do this very well along with accepting all things as they are and learning unconditional love. Lena's Mom Deryn has learnt to let go and not control as much; she is learning patience and has more empathy towards other families like hers. Deryn has definitely started to look at things from a higher perspective. Lena's sisters Juliette and Sydney have learnt to be more caring. When Juliette and Sydney were asked "what has Lena taught you" they replied "to love a baby sister and stick up for her when someone says mean things about her". Juliette's aura radiates after she had held her sister. I am so grateful for Lena; her family; her light and the lessons. Lena is a very strong soul she has gone through so much in this life time already. Just recently she had been in the hospital with a viral pneumonia; her family were asking for prayers to help with whatever journey Lena was choosing. That night I had a dream where I was holding Lena over my knee and I was rubbing my hand over her back while she was face down; then she started to release a white liquid substance that come from her lungs. I cuddled her and gave her my love. In the morning Lena started to progress and was able to go home from the hospital a few days later. I had told Deryn that Lena was of the light and she had a very high purpose here on earth. Something made Deryn go home and look up the meaning of her names. Lena means "light"; Claire her middle name means "clear, bright".

Lena makes a huge difference to all who come in contact with her.

Just before publication of this book Lena chose to leave her earthly body and return to her expansive pure light energy. A day after Lena's passing her family took pictures of themselves with friends feeling sad Lena was not a part of this. When looking at the pictures each one had a bright circle of light in them. Lena is the light she is everywhere; no longer constricted in her earthly body. Take some of the unlimited light and become more of you. Lena Claire – October 31, 2016–April 11, 2018 thank you for all you are.

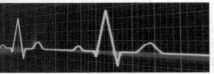

Chapter 39
Implants

I am now aware that we get implanted with thoughts and ideas from the many levels on the other side. We can get implanted with both positive and negative thoughts and even objects depending on which level they are coming from and how conscious you are.

One evening a client I had been working with to help her release some of her energy blocks called me and said "I feel a little off". I told Kaylee I would tune into her energy field. Immediately I could see that a microchip had been placed on her tongue from darker planets. I could taste the metal contamination of this microchip in my mouth. I told Kaylee that her taste buds had been affected by this; I told her what I was seeing and that I would remove the microchip. Kaylee found this interesting as she had not been able to drink her morning coffee for two days now as it tasted so awful. She had even gone to work and told the girls there who made her a cup to see if it was the water; but the coffee still tasted bad. I told Kaylee "tomorrow your coffee will taste great". The next evening Kaylee phoned me again to say I was right as her coffee tasted good again! She felt much better. This is something we would not have believed; but we had both been given the earthly validation.

While doing one to one energy work on Rick I told him I could see a magnetic file in his right knee. I told him that his knee must have been giving him trouble for the last week as I felt a burning sensation. I always feel what my client feels in my body so I know exactly what is going on with them – the feeling subsides in me as soon as I say what I feel. Rick confirmed this was true – I removed the magnetic file and his knee was fine.

One day while walking on the beach I could see something that appeared to look like a huge flat spaceship. I thought this was un-usual to see at the beach because I always think of the beach as a very positive place. This space like vessel was hovering over the rocks and people's houses; it was a very dark grey in colour and very flat. Instantly I thought it was from the darker planets and got the awareness that they were playing havoc with people's emo-tions down here on earth. I told the person who I was with "just watch out this week because this will be a week full of drama as people are going to be very emotional". This was exactly the case as people were upset with others taking everything very personally. Another time I saw one over the world; what took place that week were a lot of disasters in the world related to terrorism. The weath-er was horrific with hurricanes and storms in many places around the world. I know to look out when I see the dark, flat spaceships – there is no substance to them as they are flat – empty in side – so the more people who have awareness and light; the more this can be changed.

I find we can get implanted with information or objects to keep us in fear when we are distracted; when we get too busy we lose our awareness; when we are obsessed with one thing like work-ing out too much; having too much sex; watching too much TV; eating too much food; drinking too much; drugs, too focused on money; being obsessed with your body and your looks; involved in drama – these are all distracters to keep us unconscious. The dark energies do not want us to have awareness because if you do you will see the truth; your truth and this will send you higher in your frequency where you send out more light into the world. It is important for you to learn to be totally aware of your energy. When you feel different it is because your energy has changed. You are the only one who knows if your energy levels have lowered or gone higher – be aware!

People connect to me because they know something is going on with their energy but don't know exactly what it is. I am grateful to see beyond so I can help; but ultimately it is always the client who has to be willing to do their own work. In all my sessions I always give my clients a simple learning tool for them to take with them to help them on their journey.

Questions are good – I questioned all of this as it appeared to me. Much of this I would not have believed had my clients and I not been given the earthly validations – so then I thought well there must be something in this. Now I have had too many experiences not to believe! Remember there was a time I did not want to and was not ready to see all of this. When you are truly ready things will be presented to you.

I always work on me and look inside myself. I am aware of what my truth is and what works for my energy frequency. I am choosing for my energy to elevate to higher levels.

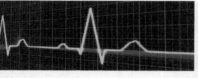

Chapter 40
Space Ships

While working on Janet I could see a space ship with her; sometimes I question what I see and I thought to myself I can't tell her that! What is this about? It continued to stay in my vision and I could see her at four years old being led into a spaceship by an extra-terrestrial being. When I said this to her Janet was surprised I would pick that up because she had said two nights earlier she had sworn she'd seen a space ship. She stared at it; she was with her son's dog that had its head cocked to one side for what seemed about ten minutes. Janet looked around where she was convinced a crowd was watching this spaceship with her but there was no one there. The air was very still and when Janet looked back the spaceship had disappeared and she could only see the moon. She doubted herself but inside knew what she had seen. She felt very alone and did not know who to tell. I helped her to clear these feelings of "loneliness" and the fear of "judgement"; the fear of being the "only one". We also had to clear "jealousy" as she had an awareness of others being jealous and not liking her if she was "different".

I had to take Janet to that point in time on to the space ship where she encountered very friendly energy. I could see the space ship at the end of a field that was sheltered by many trees. It was night time and the extra-terrestrial being wanted Janet to meet his family. I could see him taking Janet up the ramp onto the spaceship. Janet felt very safe and comfortable there. The aliens showed her everyone's house on earth and zoomed in on her house. She had been chosen to work with them as she was the "light being" and they knew she would accept them and cooperate. The other family members would have told on them. The aliens in turn would help Janet and she would help them. Somewhere society had placed these energies as dangerous and horrible, but to her she saw them as the opposite, very loving and gentle. She felt very safe with them; safer than with the people on earth. When I went up into the spaceship with Janet I felt the most unconditional love that I have ever felt so I understood why Janet would feel lonely; humans could not love to that level so Janet had been searching for that feeling her whole life. Janet was lonely for that unconditional love.

Janet no longer felt alone and was ok with carrying this warm fuzzy secret with her – her secret place and time where she could go and visit anytime; her place of comfort and security; her place of home.

A week later when Janet returned for another session she told me that during the long weekend that had just passed she had spent time with "herself" – time on her own; something she had not previously been able to do. Janet had to keep herself busy; if she'd had a day off before she made sure she had plans to do something with someone. Janet could not stand to be alone. After the "spaceship" session, Janet loved to be by herself. Janet had slept in, then got up and made herself breakfast and took it back to bed with her. Janet had breakfast in bed with herself and LOVED it! She spent the whole weekend by herself and hated when Tuesday rolled around and she had to be with other people again!

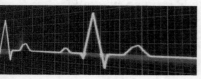

Chapter 41
Other Worlds

There are many worlds that make up this universe. When working with Tj I had the awareness that he had come from one of these "other planets – other than earth". It was a planet that I myself had not been familiar with. I was being shown a "darker" planet. In that life Tj had been "hunted" like an animal. To the men doing the chasing it was like a game, they picked the lighter energy males who were capable of doing good and threw them into the dark. These men were forced to have a microchip engraved into their skulls, so they could be tracked. The men being hunted had to think fast and had to out manoeuvre the evil. It was torturous. The men watching from screens in a cold room would just laugh at them, this gave the men doing the hunting more power so they could grow even more evil; feeding the demon inside of them.

Tj found a portal to come to earth. His whole life here was fast – he was the fastest thinker; his mind was the fastest I had ever worked with. He was a constant worrier, getting ailments and thinking they were more serious than they were. He was looking at the "bad" things and not having time to look at the "good" around him.

This made sense with his life before, knowing if he stopped to observe anything for too long he would be caught and tortured. In this life time because he had a microchip inside his skull he was still always running, being anxious – they were still tracking him and trying to find him. I had to take Tj into a meditation so he could visualise a surgery being performed on him to remove his micro chip. His wires were defused and his brain slowed down. We had to release dark energies attached to him which kept him "cold". The word "hunted" kept repeating itself. I told him he could create something from the vision that had come to him perhaps a book series, a movie or a game? He said "weird, I just saw an ad on TV for a preview of a new series called "Hunted" and I knew I had to watch it. Another earthly validation that this was true is Tj's last name is Hunt! Crazy but true! These are validations and to both of us even though this blew both our minds it made sense on a higher level.

The next session with Tj an extra-terrestrial energy channelled through me, so they could look into Tj's brain. This energy was like an E.T. grandfather, very wrinkled, his skin hard and rough. He told me that many spaceships were hovering close to earth at this moment. Tj said he had dreamt of a spaceship the night before. Tj had the awareness that the E.T. Grandfather was protecting him from his own self, from the darkness that was programmed in him from "the dark life". We had to remove the last of the strands from that life time. Tj was afraid the grandfather E.T. called Pedero would leave as he was a great comfort to him. Tj felt the E.T. Grandfather was protecting him from all the sadness. Tj was so afraid to die – he had a fear that when it was his time to die; he would go back to this past life. By clearing these energies Tj was able to move forward with just being.

Tj's brain did slow down so he could see this world in a new light. The anxiety erased from him, his blood turning to warmth. A new awakening emerging; he could now be in the light, no longer needing to hide in the dark.

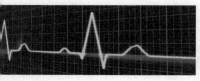

Chapter 42

Galaxies

When doing a one to one emotional releasing session on Anne Marie and releasing "love hurts", I had the vision she had belonged to the galaxies. I could see a darker galaxy which was full of women and children; their husbands were on another planet working. The husbands bought back food in the form of minerals for their wives and children. I could see that they only required one spoonful a day which started out as a black substance (it looked like very small pieces of coal) but as the people ate this substance it turned to gold which filled their whole energy field up.

In this other life Anne Marie had been with a man whom she loved so dearly but he had seven other wives with whom she felt she had to compete with. The fifth wife Sarah was so beautiful and Anne Marie could tell her husband favoured her. When Sarah fell pregnant Anne Marie was jealous. "What if the husband loved Sarah's child even more than the others?" Anne Marie became mean and overcome with jealously. She vowed to never let Sarah bear a child. When the child was born Anne Marie was the midwife and pretended the child had died. Anne Marie took the child and hid her away. When the child was three she became sick and died. Anne Marie hated herself and became even meaner. She vowed to make everyone else miserable causing grief, havoc and hurt. She told lies and manipulated the truth. Anne Marie was eventually found out. The lies all caught up with her and she was hung for her actions.

Even though Anne Marie died she left an imprint of her negative dark ways on the galaxy.

When freeing Anne Marie of the "meanness and hurt of love", we could both see the galaxy lightening up.

I had to take Anne Marie into a meditation where she had to drink mineral water to fill her body up – (something that had been her food from the galaxy, the men worked on another planet to bring home minerals for their family to survive on. My client had brought her own water from her spring well that day; it was full of minerals as Anne Marie had a life issue in this life time on Earth of not being able to absorb enough minerals into her body.) In meditation I took her to an amazing pool of water where she could swim and drink it, filling her soul and cell memory up and revitalizing her; afterwards while sitting in the sun drying a rainbow had appeared for her to dance in. Ann Marie absorbed all the magnificent energy of the rainbow. Then she went for a walk in the beautiful forest among the trees and was invited to sit down in a comfortable place. A man was coming towards her, a man who loved her every bit as much as she loved him. She was excited but anxious at the same time so I did some energetic clearings for her about receiving love and releasing the hurt of love. It was now her choice to let this amazing love in or keep it at bay because of the fear. After the clearings and change of energy she was able to let him in and hug him to feel the unconditional love and acceptance.

We were able to release the darkness that had been attached to her from the galaxy and fill her up with golden energy.

Ann Marie felt an amazing glow about her, the fore finger of both hands were buzzing like she could "zap" things.

Everything made sense to Anne Marie as she had been so hurt in this life time from love – she was mean and did not want to be. Every step forward Anne Marie takes it is towards kindness and enlightenment.

Chapter 43
Weird and Crazy

When working on Shawn I received the information that he was here from another planet. He was here to learn about humans and their emotions because he had done "bad things" where he came from. He was sent to earth to serve his sentence and punishment. He remained in his prison here, being resentful and resistant to his mission. He created more of a prison for himself here on earth putting himself through abuse and all kinds of punishments.

This was Shawn's first time on Earth so he did not know how to fit his energy into the earth's vibration. Shawn had many lifetimes on the planets. Shawn had kept himself in the prison of drugs and alcohol just to be able to cope with the energy on Earth; to try and fit in.

I told Shawn the star energy was good for him as he had come from the Star planet and he said he loved being under the stars and felt like he did not really belong here. He always felt the stars gave him good energy. He loved the night time when he would just be underneath the stars watching them.

I told Shawn I saw a ginger and white cat around him; I could see that a microchip had been planted into the cat. I felt it was to watch him so he would not escape his punishment here on Earth. I could see this cat following him around everywhere he went. Shawn thought this was crazy! Over ten years ago a "stray" ginger and white cat had shown up on his doorstep and did indeed follow him around everywhere. When the cat was older Shawn's partner brought home another abandoned cat that was also ginger and white. The old cat died and the new one took over from the old ginger cat and continued to follow Shawn around everywhere. So what seemed like just a stray cat was oh so much more!

We released resistance amongst many other things from my client. We released the prison around him, so he could have more aware-ness – to look beyond what seems like reality. Where and what is real? Is everything just an illusion?

This was indeed seemingly weird and crazy but yet it was all so familiar. The cat was an earthly validation to my client that this was indeed true to this situation. I had never seen this client before this session so how would I know about a ginger and white stray cat that followed him around everywhere? This totally resonated with Shawn and made sense to him about why he had so much trouble in this life time. With the sentence lifted from my client he was able to make better choices for himself so he could have an easier and happier life.

Chapter 44
Cell Memory Level

When doing a phone session with Lora I saw demon energy with her that was holding her back from being more. I told her that she must have been going into panic mode as I felt another planet very close above her head; it looked like one huge dark planet that had a ring around it. I could see two electric cords connected from the planet to Lora's own energy field. I told Lora that she had great awareness and could tell when someone was talking about her even from the next province. Lora confirmed that this was true. I told her this energy would come into her demonic energy field, something spirit had shown me a couple of months before when this was happening to me. People's words were like curses, making her energy field heavier and this would make her sad. It made her sad that her own children believed the manipulation of their father and did not believe that Lora was the true, loving, caring mother that she was. It made her sad that they could not see the truth. We cleared Lora's demonic energy field and she immediately felt lighter. We cleared the demon energy as well as five other entities she had hired in previous life times to keep her dull and small in her energy so she would not be seen and found by the "dark planet". I was shown a past life on the "dark planet" for Lora one where she had been a prostitute; Lora had to grovel to get men to even have sex with her as she was so dirty and felt ugly. Men would kick her and throw dirt at her; they would laugh at her for grovelling. The men would make her lick their feet for their entertainment. Women were trash to them and the men degraded them. Why is it that these men could sleep with many women and cheat on their wives and still be superior? It was about power and authority for these men. If women did that they were considered cheap and dirty. For Lora we had to clear feeling "unworthy" and feeling "worthless". We had to clear this from the cell memory level and down to the DNA strands.

In this lifetime Lora's relationship had ended and she was nervous about starting a new relationship – why? Because she was afraid she would be hurt, so we cleared that from her energy. "Why would it matter if you got hurt?" "Because I would feel worthless. I would feel that I was not wanted." This was something that had stayed in Lora's cell memory from the previous life time. Lora was afraid she would go back to the time of no one wanting her, what if she had to grovel to have sex again? Why do we need sex? To feel worthwhile?

Her affirmation: I am worthy I am, I am me, I am, I am worthy to be me, I am.

Lora had been afraid to be more than she was. What if she was found by the dark planet and had to go back to that time? We disconnected the fuse. The planet did not actually care because they had too many other people down on earth going through the same thing. I could see a few hundred that they were tracking, all going through similar emotions like Lora.

I could see a spiritual teacher with Lora, he was one of her guides; he was taking her toward enlightenment. When she dies, she herself will be a spiritual teacher; she is going to be her ex-husbands spiritual teacher because he in turn will have to go on the spiritual journey and he will see her in meditation and he will listen to her as he won't recognize her as she will be a male!

After this session Lora said she felt like she was floating she felt so good. She felt like she had been freed.

A few days later I received this message from Lora "hello, just wanted to update you on my healing. I can say with absolute certainty that the healing we had has worked. I feel worthy, like I matter. This is the first time I have felt this way, just happy with me and my life. I truly am blessed to have you in my life. Your healing was a gift. Thank you".

If something is resonating with you here, ask yourself is this a planet you came from? If it feels light it is true, if heavy then no.

There is more going on with earth than meets the eye, how deep are you willing to go?

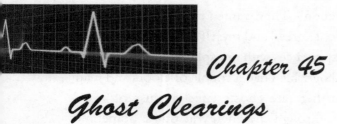

Chapter 45
Ghost Clearings

One day Steve came home from work and said the guys at work would like you to come in and see what is going on as things are happening there that are unexplainable and they think there is a ghost.

I tuned in from where I was and said I see a man on the stairs on the right hand side as you go in. I described him and said his name is Harold. Steve confirmed there had been a Harold who had worked at the sorting office fitting the description of the man and yes there were stairs on the right hand side.

The next day he went to work and told the guys and Rob confirmed the facts and the date I had given him. He also said Harold had died under the stairs at home and had been his neighbour. The guys were baffled as to how I could receive this information and see the building when I had never even entered it. I explained that I am just tuning into the energy and picking up frequencies – just like a radio.

I am that person who love to send ghosts "home", yes for many people they think it is fun and spooky but think about this, would you want to be imprisoned in a lower energy for years, even centuries?

Dave and Rob asked if I would go in one evening to clear the energy at their work. I told Steve I could do it from home but they wanted to see me in "action". They wanted me physically there so they could see what I do. I agreed and myself and four men met in the building – all had experiences with unexplainable happenings. I took a tour of the building which had a couple of floors and many different rooms. When there are ghosts I feel a sense of heaviness; it is hard to walk through the energy at times. Sometimes my stomach will flip and I can get a headache as I am aware that some do not want me to clear them because this is the place they have known for so long. Harold liked to be at the sorting office because he felt useful there. He had died only a couple years after his retirement. He did not feel useful at home. His daughter had committed suicide and they were at different levels on the other side but thankfully I was able to reunite them and send them both to a peaceful place.

I went around the building burning sage (you do not really need that to clear the energy but that is how some people have to receive it) the sage helps clear out negative energy. I light tea lights and place them where I think the portals are (I see them as open tubes of energy where spirits can come and go) or where most of the ghosts are. As I went to the lunch room I saw a grumpy man sitting in the corner. I told Rob the man was miserable and described how the man looked. Rob said "he was miserable his name was George and he made my life miserable!" This man held on to a lot of grief in his life time on earth, hence the misery. I continued to go around – there was a women spirit who had been rich but had her dignity taken away from her, she had blue eyes and blonde wavy hair – I knew she had not belonged to the sorting office. That is when I learnt from the men that before it had been a sorting office it had been a hospital. I felt many spirits there some from long ago.

Before it was a hospital it had been a work house so everything began to make sense.

I had to place a candle on someone's work station; interestingly enough it was Dave's who was one of the men present. He had experiences that happened to him when he was there later in the evening. Most of the men had the experiences when they were there by themselves working or only a few men around, mostly in the evenings. This is because during the day when lots of people are around it is noisier, lighter; you are feeling the presence of the earth humans around you so it is a distraction. When hardly any-one is around there is less noise and less distractions.

I was in the kitchen which had a room with the toilet right beside. I said "there is a lot of spirits in here" I felt sick. Rob confirmed that one day as he had gone to the toilet and come out there was a waste bin and the lid had been taken off and placed on the counter.

When I had finished putting the candles around and cleansing the space we went outside for about fifteen minutes. I see the spirits leaving in a vortex energy going out of the building up into the universe. (You don't want to interrupt the flow of the energy leav-ing – hence going outside) Many were leaving but George was be-ing stubborn. I called upon spirits who had crossed over already to come help as well as angels and any other loving beings. George's mothers came to help and she put her arm around him very gently and he cried he had so much grief inside of him that I let him stay awhile so that he would not have to take that grief with him. He eventually went with his Mum.

As we were outside I was feeling a grandmother very strong for one of the men. I described her and said she was from the father's side. Malcolm confirmed it was his grandmother. I told him she wanted him to know that she is always with him. She indicated he had a young son whom she was also with. Malcolm confirmed this. She wanted him to know that he must open his heart a little more;

his son was just like him and kept his emotions close. They would both go through a bit of a hard time, he had to take some chances and go beyond his bubble. He understood all this completely with what was going on in his life. Malcolm had been going through a difficult time and he felt better knowing that he and his son had someone to watch over them.

When we went back inside the energy felt calmer. I could now walk through the place and especially on the stairs with ease. We checked the candles and the men were so surprised to see that the three spots where I felt the ghosts the most had completely burnt down. It was really interesting as two were lit at the exact same time; the one in the toilet completely dissolved while the one next to it in the kitchen burnt about half way. This was a good validation for the men to see.

To me I was very grateful for these men to have an open mind, to be willing to go beyond. Rob had heard a man's voice a couple of weeks before calling his name but no one was there. He in turn trusted his instincts enough to ask Steve if I could come to the building. After he said "it makes sense I think it was Harold calling saying that he knew he had been "locked up" for too long – it was as if he knew I could ask Steve to ask you to help."

No one at the sorting office had really known this was happening but the next day after this had been spoken about a few other stories had come out.

Many had thought the radio was on when it was not. While I was clearing the energies the TV was off and the postmen all indicated that it was on all the time! Many felt they were being watched.

Scott sent me a photo of three long scratches on his arm. He had been alone working one Christmas, he had not brushed up against anything and the scratches appeared. It had happened two Christmases in a row.

Al said that he was once working an afternoon shift. The building had been locked so he opened it and then locked the door behind him. He went into the front office and started doing some work on the computer. In this front office there is a sliding glass security hatch in the door. All of a sudden a lady pokes her head through this hatch and he realized someone was there and asked her "how did you get in here?" She indicated with her hand – not saying anything. He said "you're not allowed in here you have to get out" and he put her in the front lobby, locking the door behind her. The front lobby has a door to the outside which was also locked. Then he looked out into the lobby from the serving hatch and she was gone, completely vanished in between two locked doors which she could not have unlocked! When the postmen asked him what she looked like he described her with blonde hair and blue eyes exactly like the women I had seen!

So to Rob, Steve, Malcolm and Dave thank you for making a difference, thank you for helping to send these ghosts to freedom!

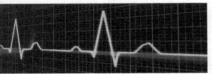

Chapter 46
Soul Shadow

P amela contacted me to say she had felt she had something in her house and could I clear it? When I tuned in I could see a dark silhouette of a young male, he kept hiding; the word "torture" came up for her.

At that moment I was told she had to get a dark green candle to light when I came to her house to do the clearing for her.

On the day of the reading/clearing I realized Pamela had a lot of energy attached to her from her Dad, she needed to heal issues from him and to let go of his beliefs that she had absorbed into her energy. I asked her "Are you willing to release energy blocks related to being told what to do?"

Pamela had a past life in Germany where she was a male and had to torture prisoners – if she did not do this she would have been tortured herself. As a young boy in that past life she had been taught by her Dad to be "strong" by being strong it meant you bullied people; you hit them, you tortured them. Pamela's Dad wanted a strong boy not someone who was weak; he had been beaten by his Dad himself -he needed to be strong, not weak – this was the "shadow of the soul".

How do you get rid of the "shadow of your soul"? Everyone is different and Pamela had to catch her shadow and hug him – she had to tell him she loved him, he had no choice to do what he did otherwise he would have been beaten to death – she had to forgive him and he had to forgive himself! When she did this she started to cry as it was so freeing, the shadow disappeared, she let go of the attachment that had been stopping her from going forward.

Pamela had to write a forgiveness letter to her Dad in this lifetime as she always had to do what he told her to do, if she did not do what he told her then she would be punished; even though her Dad does not know how to forgive himself Pamela can give him the gift of releasing in the cell memory. As she forgives him, his energy will also free and when it is his time to pass he can have an easier transition to the other side.

In turn, Pamela will be free to start living for her, to start loving herself for who she really is instead of living for her Dad. She had always thought I can start being myself when my Dad dies – why wait? Face the fear. In Pamela's cell memory she was afraid of all the conflict and punishment – afraid to fail, afraid of the consequences. Pamela can now cut the attachments, setting herself free, allowing herself to go higher in her vibration.

Write a letter to yourself, forgiving you, burn it in the green candle – for your soul's journey – so you can go to higher levels when you die. Is there anyone else you need to forgive? If so write them a letter and burn it in the colour of your choice. You might want yellow for change and happiness or turquoise and light blue for peace and tranquillity. Trust yourself. We are only aware and conscious of about 5% of what is inside of us – the other 95% is hidden away in our cell memory and DNA – to be revealed when we are ready. We cannot remember everything we have done in previous life-

umes. We all have a shadow to our soul; release and forgive yourself whether you remember what you need forgiving for or not.

Here is an exercise you can try — sit down with your eyes closed — place your hand over your heart and say "I love you, I am sorry, I forgive you, I love you." Repeat this until you can feel it in your soul.

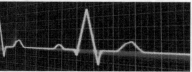

Chapter 47
The Clearing of Animals

One day when having an emotional release session with Keith anger came up. I told him that it was not worth releasing any more anger from his energy because the anger was associated with his house he had moved into. I knew that if I continued to release any anger from his energy field each time he went home he would be moody, irritated and angrier as he had negative energy in his home. I needed to release what was in his home so it would not affect Keith.

I knew his house had been called the slaughter house but I was confused because the image I could see was of a court yard with a shire horse and a man. The man was controlling and he was in control of this horse. I told Keith to me it did not make sense to see a horse when I knew it was a slaughter house where he lived. He replied that it did make sense because the house we are in was the old coach house; downstairs was the stables where the horses were kept. The place opposite which they had converted into a holiday home was the old slaughter house. I told him I would come up and clear the space for him.

As I approached his house through the courtyard I felt an intense energy wash over me. This was the courtyard that I had seen during my previous sessions working on him. I could also see the man and the horse walking around! I felt an intense heaviness in front of one building; all over the courtyard was a thick energy that was hard to walk through. At the end of the courtyard there was a gravel drive leading to two more houses but unlike the heaviness of the first building they felt light and I did not feel the ghost energies around there. Keith later confirmed that the gravel area had been a field where the animals roamed so nothing "bad" would have happened there. When I walked into Keith's house immediately I felt overwhelmed with how many energies were there. I can honestly say that I have never walked into a house where there were so many.

Keith and Amy showed me around. My head was aching and I felt physically sick with so many energies around me. We sat down at the kitchen table for a cup of tea and a chat when I was almost knocked off my seat by a spirit dog. I told them that there was a collie dog in the house. They had no knowledge of a dog living there but later asked one of the previous owners of the land about it and they said yes that there had once been a collie dog called Mandy living there. This was a validation to them that what I had seen was true.

Keith also showed me a photo he was able to acquire from someone whose family had owned the land at one time. In the picture was the man I had seen with the horse. He was an angry man who wanted to tell people what to do, he wanted control. He sold horses and cows to the barracks in town where the soldiers were. He wanted the money and wanted the say. His energy was a little stubborn to go but eventually he did.

We started to clear the energies from upstairs, every room had an energy in it; in one of the bedrooms there was a portal where energies could come and go. You could tell where the portal was because it was freezing; every other room in the house was hot. Amy's son who had been sleeping; got up to be a part of this clearing. I could see that Amy's son had energies around him. Amy had thought he was sick as he was sleeping all the time but I felt strongly it was the energies keeping him down so he could "avoid" life and his feelings. We continued clearing the space and energies. I closed the portal – where spirits and energy's come and go in the room that was freezing as this was a contribution to the house to do this. When closing a portal I always ask if it is for the highest good to close it – as not all portals should be closed. While the energies were clearing we went across to the "slaughter house". This was Keith and Amy's favourite holiday home but I felt heavy energy in the hall way down stairs and told them what I was feeling, they said "that was where the cows were slaughtered." I felt there were some cows still in spirit there and because they had been killed so quick did not know they were dead – just like humans can be. This was a learning lesson for me as I did not think that cows would be ghosts! I cleared the energy in this house and went next door to another holiday home which had really good energy. I believe that had been a storage shed, so again nothing "bad" would have happened there. We stayed in this one while the spirits and energies were clearing in the other two places. I could see cows going up in a vortex energy from the slaughter house, great big cows! I myself felt amazed by this as I would not have believed it had I not seen them go. When I felt that the cows had all gone we went back inside where it was calm and very easy to walk through the entrance way where the cows had been slaughtered. It was a very peaceful feeling.

When we returned to Keith and Amy's house again it was a lot easier to walk through the energy. My headache was gone and I did not feel overwhelmed. Now when there are so many spirits and energies to clear it can be hard to clear them all at once but I felt like many of them had gone. When we checked the candles that I had placed in every room they had all been burnt right down – I had never seen this before, usually only some of them burn all the way down. The only one that only burnt half way was the one in the bathroom and I believe this happened so that Keith, Amy and the family could see it was not just the candles.

The house was quieter although I felt something still around Amy's son. Interestingly enough a couple days later Amy called to say her son was having trouble sleeping. Keith was brilliant, he was calm and happy, as was Amy's daughter and herself but her son was scared. When her son had his friend over, he went into the bathroom where he got scratched by "something". Recalling when we did the cleanse, that was the only room where the candle did not go all the way down; sometimes energies can hide; sometimes you need to do it twice. Sometimes you have to clear that person of the attachments and entities around them.

A few days later I cleansed her son in a one to one energy session.

Amy told me after the clearing she felt good. She said that she had felt funny about me for a few weeks before the clearing as if she was being told to stay away from me. She said that the feeling had gone away now and she realized the energies were trying to prevent her from having me there to clear them. It is as if somehow they know what is going to happen and know I am coming to clear them. We had tried to arrange this clearing session three times but each time something happened and we had to postpone it. I have done this enough times now that I am aware of what the "ghosts/ spirits/energies/entities" are doing. They try to scare you and can try to stop you. I would have been scared of them in the past but I am now aware that I am stronger than they are and I am not afraid to send them to a higher place where they will be happier – they are just unaware and can't see the light from where they are.

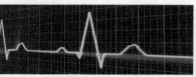

Chapter 48
The Demon Within

While reading a young males aura I could see he had a dark energy attached to him. He had been sleeping all the time so had thought there must be something wrong with him. I told him there was nothing physically wrong, he was very sensitive and he was trying to NOT be aware of the energies around him. With sleeping so much he could then avoid life, avoid himself and the energies he could feel. I could see he had an energy in his bedroom; it was in the right hand upper corner. It appeared to me like a dark speck at first but then grew like a spiders web until this dark demon appeared and filled up his bedroom.

I went to clear his space and afterwards he admitted that he could not sleep anymore he was so aware of someone watching him. He was scared. I taught him that he was stronger in his mind than anyone. He could use his mind to kill these psychic vampires with light and love. I taught him how to see a light inside him and grow it all throughout his body, then beyond his body into the room and grow it bigger than the building and keep growing it until it expanded out into the universe and beyond. It is important to keep your energy in expansion. When it is contracted negative things can happen and energies can attach.

His great grandmother on his Dad's side came through in spirit to explain why this was happening to him. She said he could learn from this experience and that she was also with him and to not be afraid. For although "bad" things were around if she was not helping him things would be far worse. I could see this demon figure around him and tried to clear it but it was very stubborn and hard to get rid of. We cleared entities from his energy and he was aware that he had nine of them, as well as some other energies that had served their purpose. However, the demon was persistent. I asked questions about the demon energy and looked further inside of him before realizing that my client had been the demon energy in a past life. He had killed and tortured people and loved it! He fed on the pure pleasure of seeing the fear in people's eyes! Now in this life he had come back to help and heal people, to learn a different side of things. He had to forgive himself and his previous actions. As he did this the demon energy dissolved away and my client shed two levels of skin (I am shown two layers of skin falling away energetically from their body so I know the clients energy field has changed). He walked away a different person; he was shining brighter and his skin colour no longer deathly white.

The next day he told me that he had slept peacefully all night.

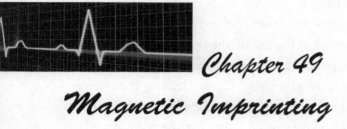

Chapter 49
Magnetic Imprinting

Richard and Christine asked me to go to their house so I could see what was going on. They felt coldness inside their house and many negative things were happening to them in their lives.

In viewing Richard and Christine's house there were certain rooms where I felt a lot of energy. I described the image of a man and Richard said "that's who we bought the house from." I told him that he was a miser and argumentative, especially in the bedroom where I was. Richard said that the bedroom that we were in used to be an office for the man's business. The man had apparently double crossed his business partner and that is why in the end he sold the house. Richard himself was having trouble in his business. Even though the man they had bought the house from was still alive he had left his magnetic imprinting in the home. Magnetic imprinting is a cloud of negative energy. For example think of when someone has an argument and you walk in ten minutes later you can feel the heaviness of the energy, it is the magnetic imprinting of the argument. Even though the argument is complete and done the energy is left behind. Even Richard himself had grumpy, argumentative times in his home. He did not like it but it was as if sometimes he could not help it. We cleared the energies in the house and I told Christine to make sure she got a crystal to place in the window of the room where the office used to be. I was drawn to a door which I felt had a lot of negative imprinting on and Richard and Christine confirmed it was an original feature of the house. The parts of the house that I felt were good were the parts that they had renovated. They had put in their good energy. Upon clearing the negative energy the house felt calm and peaceful. Christine put a crystal up in the bedroom and bought crystal lights for the hallways which created beautiful rainbow prisms. This created so much more lightness and lifted the house to a happier level.

Karen had heard about my work and what I did and decided that she needed to come and see me for a session. I could see her Great Great Grandmother with her on her Dads side of the family but I could also see the same energy in Karen. I could hear the Great Great Grandmother saying she had been raped by her Uncle, she had felt shame and unworthiness. She felt unworthy to receive anything good, anything that made her happy, and any extra money; she had kept the rapes a secret her whole life out of fear – fear from the Uncle – fear that her "dirty" secret would be found out, so she locked it away inside herself. The grandmothers energy also said what I was seeing was a magnetic imprinting of her, of how she was when she died; she had reincarnated into Karen. So Karen had her great great grandmother's cell memory inside of her and had gone through similar experiences herself. Karen confirmed that she had but had also kept them a secret because she thought no one would believe her so she hid them away deep inside of her soul. Karen could not believe I would know this as she had never told anyone about her sexual trauma. When releasing emotion with Karen she could feel herself in her body and then out of her body and then in and out. I said well that would make sense seeing you are clearing from your soul and the magnetic imprinting of your Great Great Grandmother's soul. You are two within the same. Karen was here to free the cell memory, to stand up for her and speak up. It was time for her to take back her inner power having allowed others to take it from her. Karen said the family member who had committed the sexual offenses against her, had cancer three times in this life time and eventually died. Was this caused from keeping the secret? Did this cause the dis-ease inside?

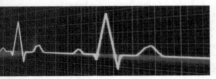

Chapter 50
Infinite Love

A young male called Ryan had come to me for a reading. He was very nervous as he had never been introduced to this before so therefore was skeptical.

Ryan's Great Grandmother on his Moms side appeared first telling him she had held him as a baby, this he understood and knew was true. His Grandfather from his Dad's side came through to say hello to him also. He had been very close to him. Two young people appeared with him, one a friend and one a girlfriend both had died in car accidents. His girlfriend Stacey came through to tell him she had been speeding because she had been angry with her boss. Ryan knew this was true as the last text he received from her said "she was mad at her boss". She told him that it was her time to go as she had learnt her piece with this earthly world; he had to stay. She told him that she knew he was contemplating suicide to be with her but he should not do this because it would take them longer to be together. He would go to a different level in the after world if he did this.

Stacey also said "they would have their next life time together where they would meet at fifteen and be childhood lovers. They would get married and have three children and they would live in the house they had already talked about in this life time, the one with the porch." This was his girlfriend's house in this life time that was falling down and they talked about fixing it up so they could live in it – Ryan still intended to fix it up in this lifetime.

His girlfriend told him that they had a past life together where she was married to someone else and he had tried to steal her from her husband and have an affair with her in hopes she would leave her husband for him but her husband had been too controlling and she went back to him. It was not their time yet. Ryan had to pay the Karma back to do with "stealing".

Stacey told Ryan she would send him a baby and there would be a few relationships for him – all soul mates teaching him soul lessons. He would not be completely satisfied though because she had left a deep imprint in his heart because she was his infinite love!

Ryan came to me because a friend recommended me. He was desperate to communicate with his girlfriend he felt lost as if he did not know how to live without her. She had accepted him, allowed him to be himself when no one else seemed to understand him.

Everyone else had wanted him to get on with things – he needed to get on with things! It helped when I told him that everyone heals and grieves differently, it was ok to do it his way. He will never get over it – he will just learn to cope with it in a new way.

Ryan wanted to kick and scream at the world – why didn't it understand? Why had this happened to him? He had not even had the chance to ask Stacey to marry him yet –how he wished he had.

Every night Stacey told him that she kissed him goodnight, for him to close his eyes and feel her – she will kiss him good night every night for the rest of his life. She will be the one to meet him when his time is done here on earth and they will come back to earth one more time to live their lives out fully together; where they can be truly together again.

He understood, no longer skeptic understanding that suicide was no longer the answer for him, she was his infinite love and would be worth the wait and the sacrifice.

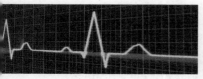

Chapter 51

Suicide

For many people death is hard to cope with but suicide is so hard to comprehend. There are so many unanswered questions and emotions involved.

We must always remember that we are "souls" in a human body in this time and place at this very moment. We are all having an earthly experience; that is what we chose to do. For many earthlings we do not remember where we have been or who we have been before; we chose to come here on earth to learn about emotions and to have an emotional experience. We all have so many emotions and in a time of death and especially in suicide so many of them come into play. We are all on our journey called "life".

I have dealt with many people who have chosen suicide and from what I have observed from them, they chose to be the ones to commit suicide so others could learn about their deep embedded emotions, some of them so hidden that only a suicide could bring them out.

Some spirits have told me that they planned their death before they came to earth, they planned this with you, so you could learn and they could teach; it is not for you to take personally, it was not your fault it was not anything you did. It is for you to learn about the emotions of guilt, anger, shame, sadness, grief and even spirituality – many of you would never have looked at that part of your life if this had not happened.

Somewhere, somehow they know their time is up and they have to do this, many have to be intoxicated so someone or something else can take over them, because otherwise they could not have done it.

There are many types of suicides that I have worked on, some have crossed over immediately and some take a long time.

Some I have personally helped to cross over so they can be at peace and not in the world of turmoil – I call it the in between worlds, they are not on earth but not in heaven either; they are on a lower energy plane. You can tell because anything that is of a lower vibration sucks the energy out of you and you can feel exhausted after working with these energies.

Once these energies have crossed we must honour them knowing they have done their journey for this moment in time here on earth. They can now be with us on a higher level guiding us, helping and protecting us. We must release them and let them go; so they and as well as us in turn can be free.

It is so shocking when we hear of someone that has committed suicide – it sends a tidal wave of emotions through life itself. Oh my gosh how could this have happened? We are shocked that we could not see it, if only we knew maybe we could have saved them. The truth is we are not meant to save them, if we were then we would have. It was their choice, their journey ended – for this moment on earth. We do need to accept the situation, for you will meet them again in another dimension at another time. When it is time for your earthly journey to end they could be the one meeting you, taking you to another level.

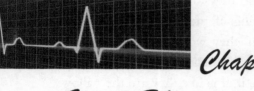

Chapter 52
Your Shadow

Sometimes in your hour of need when you just can't take it anymore when you feel like you are breaking, you reach out to someone; anyone – no one is there, it is just an empty echo. No one picks up the phone; the few who would get it are working or unavailable. You are left alone with your shadow. The deep cold shadow of your soul; it is crawling out of your body. You don't understand what is happening only that your soul is stretching out, breaking free. What will it take for this process to be pain free? What will it take for you to understand why and what exactly is happening to you? You have two ways to go here, you can take your life so the pain can go away or you can breathe one gentle tiny breath at a time. Focus on someone who would be devastated by your death, the one who needs you, and the one who you make a difference to. In your mind grab their hand, feel the warmth of their heart as they embrace you. Filling you up with light, kindness and caring. Even the strongest of people sometimes needs someone; someone to embrace them so they do not have to do this journey alone.

I think of your beautiful face and your warm loving heart then I fade into the darkness of my soul and you start to fade away. I am so very sorry for all the hurt that I have caused, I wonder if others are sorry? I wonder if they would be sorry for all the nasty things they said, for all the lies they told so they looked good. I wonder if they would have said all those things if they did not think I was such a strong person? I wonder if they would have manipulated my children and taken them away. When a strong person gets abused over and over and they take it, it is like they are the willow tree, they can bend and bend time and time again and then all of a sudden SNAP! They break – like a tree branch thrown to the floor.

I wonder if they will care a little more if I am not here?

 Broken I start to take the pills beside my bed; things start to slow down it is like everything is in slow motion. I can feel my heart slowing I know I am nearing the end and then from somewhere I can hear – I somehow sense that my door is being kicked in – I can hear lots of yelling – the colours are fading and I can hardly hear anything anymore – my strength is being taken away from me – I can feel my heart slowing down, getting slower and slower until it is gone...

From somewhere I see a bright light it feels so warm like nothing I have ever felt before; a man stands in front of me, he cares about me. I want to stay with him I reach for his hand so he can take me with him but he tells me it is not my time and I must go back – I have things to teach and things to learn. I must keep his energy with me and remember his loving touch; he will guide me for the rest of my time here on earth. Slowly I feel heaviness, the darkness around me once more – why am I in this cold place again? Is this my punishment for being so bad? Why was I not good enough to go? Why wouldn't they take me? Even they did not want me – I am so angry! I feel agitated – why do I have all these tubes hooked up to me? I rip them out and then ouch feel a stab and then I don't remember. I only know that when I wake up I am in the place I started from – or am I?

Chapter 53
Cold Energy of Suicide

As the rain is pouring down here in England and I am typing on my computer I feel a cold shiver running along my arm, oh no, this happens to me when a spirit has not crossed over. Somewhere deep inside I know a lady has committed suicide.

For a few weeks now I have felt the upheaval of the universe. When I look at the sea it speaks to me. A couple of weeks ago when I had gone to watch the waves; I knew people's emotions were in turmoil. The sea was a dirty colour, swirling the sand around underneath the waves. I thought this is just like people's emotions – they are all coming to the surface – some are ugly and hard to deal with, some have been pushed down for so very long, some we have not really been aware of – but now is the time to deal with them. It is a time for people to be truthful. Instead of shoving our emotions down and pretending we are fine, we need to share our feelings – we are not alone, many people at this moment are fighting their emotions and not understanding why they feel so sad.

Later I was in a shop buying a birthday card when I came across a small yellow duck, a sign from Nick (who is in spirit). He always comes forward to help someone where there is a suicide involved. The yellow duck also had white daisies on it, a sign from my Gran so I knew she was also helping with love. This situation would need a great deal of it.

I felt very heavy in the energy around me, a sadness came over me, I knew someone again had committed suicide but not sure who. On my way home I bumped into a friend who was associated with Nick and understood all about the spiritual work I did. I felt compelled to tell him that someone had committed suicide and Nick would be helping that soul to cross over. Even though I have done this work for twenty years sometimes you still doubt and think what am I telling him this for? What if we don't find out who this is? Then somewhere you trust because the feelings are too strong to ignore. Nick has been working with me now for about seven years so I am getting to know his energy very well.

A couple of days later I ran into my friend again and he validated that there was indeed a female energy who had committed suicide. She was connected to Nick's sister; he passed the message on about crossing the soul over. I know when the time is right Nick and my Gran will guide me to help the family who very much need love at this time and to help the female spirit to cross over where they can all have the peace they deserve.

When I type the word deserve I am aware that she did not think she deserved happiness, she is carrying a lot of guilt with her. She will remain stuck because of the "guilt" she felt, the guilt her family is also carrying around with them. As you are reading this please know that every single person on this earth deserves happiness no matter what has happened during their life here on earth. It is time to communicate our true feelings so we can free the pain in our hearts, so we can free our souls.

I know that I will have to facilitate the freeing of her pain, when she and her family are ready.

Everyone one and every soul is different, it will all happen when everything is in perfect alignment.

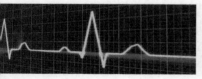

Chapter 54
Soul Brother

While doing a reading for Shawna her "soul brother" came through. This soul brother had come through for her before at one of my message evenings and I was aware he had become entwined with suicide although he had not yet crossed over; right then and there we crossed him over so he was no longer caught between the different worlds.

The soul brother had come through for Shawna on one other occasion when I and another medium sat for her and the wife of the soul brother. He was able to communicate much clearer to the family now that he had crossed over. Around the soul brother there had been many rumours and gossip about his death and he wanted to let his family know that he loved them very much and the circumstances around his death did not matter. Just because he chose suicide did not mean he did not love his family.

In the reading he had said that he had planned his death before he had come to earth and that the events leading up to his death had to take place so he would take his life. He had some negative things happen to him and he had a negative attachment to him which I call an entity. He had hired this entity to help him with this act called suicide before he even came to earth as he knew he would not actually be able to do this to his loving family. This soul brother was a good man, full of love and fun; he knew he would opt out of this if he had his choice. So the entity helped him with this, he helped him write letters to his family and plan his death. He helped the soul brother keep his word as he had promised before he came into this life time so everyone else could learn from the lessons attached to this. The soul brother had said that he had agreed to this because of his Dad; he had previous lifetimes with him and his Dad was always afraid of death and had not learnt to embrace it. Everyone dies it is a fact on earth; the human body dies although your soul evolves so there is nothing to be afraid of. He told me his Dad was still afraid to die and the soul brother had told him he would go before him so he would be there to help him to the other side. If his Dad died with fear he would remain a ghost for an eternity; he would be there to take his Dads hand so he could pull his energy through the realms of time.

Now the soul brother had been released from his "prison" his purpose at this point in time was to help others in the in between world go to the higher lighter realms. He helps people on earth with death; the ones who are afraid to die; the ones who are not spiritual and do not believe in the afterlife of the soul. He stops them from being ghosts and guides them to the level of where their soul needs to go. He takes them to safety.

The soul brother chose sacrifice. He sacrificed his actually family; his loving wife and children for the good of all.

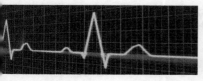

Chapter 55

Loneliness

A client I worked with had lost her cousin to suicide. This was something that had unsettled Lisa to her core. The family had not seen this coming at all! Lisa herself had thought she was in tune with people and their feelings because she was sensitive herself so how could she have not seen this?

When I tuned into Claire's spirit I picked up loneliness with her. I said that because Claire felt so lonely inside she was actually pushing her family and friends away. Claire had started to go inside herself becoming the introvert, allowing her energy to contract which made her sad and the loneliness even more apparent. Claire made excuses so she would not have to see people, which made her family feel even worse following her death, even though Claire was the one who had pushed everyone away.

I explained that Claire had not crossed over yet and that was why Lisa had been feeling so uneasy. In order to help Claire cross over, under my guidance, I told Lisa to light a large white candle. Lisa then called in her loving Mom who had passed on to help guide this process and all the other loved ones she could think of that would help with this situation. Lisa reminisced about some of the fun times they'd had together and the laughter they had shared. She recalled many shared memories with lots of family members so Claire would not feel lonely. Lisa asked Claire to seek out the family members who had crossed before her and to take their hands because she did not have to make this journey alone. Claire called them all to come to Lisa and help her to cross to the light. Lisa pulled all their love to Claire so everyone from all light levels helped to cross Claire over. After Claire had crossed Lisa felt ease all around her; the energy of uneasiness lifted – a sense of calm filled her up.

If you notice someone around you today who seems to have withdrawn from life reach out to them; phone them; knock on their door; send them a card; invite them out for a coffee; send them a note of a beautiful memory you have together; send them flowers; anything you can think of. If that person in turn chooses to keep you shut out then you must know that you did all you could. Feel good that you at least reached out to them. Everyone has choices; every choice is your own. Everyone has their journey to do; each unique; each person doing their journey their way. We might not understand everyone's individual journey but we must honour them as it is for the higher purpose of all; the purpose of the afterlife; the bigger picture of life itself.

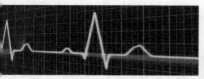

Chapter 56
The Dis-ease of Anorexia

L aura was one of my clients and she private messaged me through face book. She had felt a spirit visit with her but the contact had made her feel uneasy and she thought she was going crazy. To me this was not crazy she was just opening up to the other side – all levels of spirit. Laura got the name Hannah for the spirit who came through. Laura asked me what she was supposed to do with this information. "What should I do if she contacts me again?" I told Laura to ask what it was that Hannah required from her. I told Laura not to be afraid because this was a new lower energy coming in; an energy she was not accustomed to feeling – there was no need to feel scared because she was a gentle spirit. Laura felt the gentleness of Hannah also, but she still felt uneasy, the uneasiness of someone being around her watching her.

Laura was woken by a sensation of heaviness around her neck. This was Hannah; Laura discovered that Hannah had hung herself when she was eighteen years old. Hannah suffered from anorexia. Laura was still unsure how to deal with this information. Laura felt that Hannah had not moved on and that she was scared and wanted to be with her. This made sense because the night before Laura started sensing Hannah around her Laura had been looking at a picture of herself on line. It had been taken when she had also been suffering from anorexia. They had a shared connection.

I told Laura she could cross Hannah over because she understood her pain. Maybe there were still some things that Laura needed to heal from that time in her own life. Laura had been angry when she had anorexia. Laura hated herself and others; she hated them for interfering and telling her what to do. Laura had been at dis-ease with herself and life. Laura had been low and suicidal. She understood why Hannah would take her life. When we are at dis-ease with ourselves, others and life it can physically turn into an actual disease within our bodies. This is why it is so important to heal any emotions inside of ourselves.

I told Laura to light a candle and talk to Hannah, to tell her she understands her and to forgive her. She needed to tell Hannah to forgive herself. Laura lit the candle and asked her grandmother to help. I helped Laura with the process over the internet link. We both sent love to Hannah and both said our own things. We both hugged Hannah showing her unconditional love and acceptance. Laura told her to go to the light. I could see her go and Laura felt herself relax and then felt like crying – which is a release, a relief that Hannah had crossed over.

Well done Laura, you helped send a beautiful soul home.

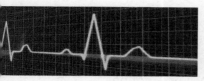

Chapter 57
An Angry Bull

I had heard of a suicide relating to close friends of mine. I could feel the shock this had brought, the heaviness of emotion, and the disbelief. How could he have done this? How could he have left us? How could he have left his children? All the sorrow, the anger, the distress of not being able to think and get your head around it, the sheer exhaustion of it all.

What is the purpose of it all? There is always a higher purpose that we cannot see at the time – it will have a ripple effect to many people – for me I would not have written this book if he had not taken his life. So maybe he sacrificed his life to save others -we might not ever know until the afterlife.

For me when I tuned into Andrews energy he was very angry, angry like a mad bull; even as I sit here typing this his energy is freezing cold. It has only been a few days since he died and he has not crossed yet. I feel he has to calm down first, he will when he is exhausted. He does not know where he is – "Why can no one see him?" he asks he wants to get to his children but they cannot see him or hear him. "Why not?" he screams!!!!!!

I feel I cannot cross him over yet because he is too angry. I know I must see his friend Clive in a couple of days when they are ready as they are exhausted themselves. Together we will do a private ceremony to send Andrew into the light of love where he can be at peace.

I know when he crosses over it will feel warm again for them and us. His loved ones here will be able to see him and feel him around them as he helps them on their earthly journey of emotions.

We must let go otherwise we are only holding ourselves back from going higher, when we can't let go we are hurting, wanting to control the situation but it is out of our hands, it has happened and we cannot change that. We need to let go so we can be happier, but most people feel, am I allowed to be happy again? I shouldn't be happy when something like this has happened – if we do laugh or feel happy for any length of time we feel guilty so we make ourselves sad again. When this happens we are resisting change, the change that has already taken place. We think we have control but the truth is we don't. The best thing you can do for everyone is to let go. It does not mean you don't care.

A month or so later I felt Andrew was ready to cross. I asked his friend Clive to come to my place so we could do a private ceremony. I told Clive to bring three pieces of music with him, one to honour his friend in the past, present and future. We lit a candle for Andrew and Clive spoke about their great friendship and how much he missed him. Andrew's energy came closer to us, I told Clive that I could see Andrew had been in a meadow – he confirmed that was where Andrew had killed himself – and then Andrew lay in an exhausted heap on the floor. We picked him up off the floor and Clive literally had to hug him, it was very moving to see the deep love between two great friends.

We played the first song that Clive had chosen "one hundred years" to me this validated that if we had not crossed him over he would have indeed been a ghost for one hundred years. To honour his past Clive said how he felt about him and spoke about some of the good times they shared together. Then we played a song called "Faith" to honour the present where we talked about forgiveness, this made sense because a lot of faith was needed in the present for all involved. Then we played "From the edge of the deep green sea" to represent the future; to me this indicated that Andrews soul would rise again and would heal from this earthly life. This was to honour Andrew, so he could see how much he was loved; this was to set him free so he could move forward easily. I told Clive Andrew was ready to go. I told him that someone had come to meet Andrew, he looked exactly like him. Clive was speechless as he said that Andrew had a twin brother who had died at birth and no one really knew about that. As Andrew went to his brother and the beautiful light, a sense of warmth filled the room, an amazing feeling of peace. It was a moment that only Clive, Andrew, his brother and I will know about and experience. Clive has felt Andrew around him many times since.

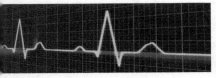

Chapter 58

Broken

The shock of Jamie committing suicide rampaged through our little community. Oh no, his poor family. Only a year ago Jamie's' cousin had been killed in a snowmobiling accident and now they have lost Jamie. Two sisters had lost their sons. How does a family handle another devastating blow? I had already helped the one sister Marilyn out with messages from her son Kyle after he had passed and felt very strongly that I had to help Roberta and her family with the passing of Jamie. Sometimes it is so hard especially when you know the family, I felt sick for them, I felt so bad that they had to go through all this pain and suffering. When I tuned into Jamie's energy I knew he had not crossed over yet. Kyle was around me very strong and I knew he would guide this process. Jamie had been angry and confused with what had been happening in his life. He was mad at what someone had done to him and wanted a little revenge. He was confused and mixed up in his head. He could not think straight any more. He did not want to be here in this "shit hole" anymore. He was mad at the whole world right now. Everyone was trying to tell him what to do, well what about what he wanted? He did not even know what he wanted any more – he took a stiff drink and then some more – the burning in his throat felt good. He felt meanness inside of him it was coming up from inside his stomach somewhere deep down; he had the image of Russian roulette, playing with guns, and he went and got his gun. He felt he had been that mean gangster in a past life, he could see it now; he loved the feeling of power, seeing someone cower when he pulled that trigger against their head. He wasn't really mean in this present life time sometimes maybe he was even too nice. He let people do things to him so he would not lose them – maybe it was because he was mean before and he had to learn to be a different way? He drank a little more, he could see so many men around him they wanted him to play Russian roulette; they wanted him to pull the trigger. That is what he could see a scene from so long ago; he was in another life time. A life time of big cigars, gambling, boozing and women – a lifetime of trying to prove yourself to the gangsters – proving you were a man! It did not matter who you hurt along the way, it was about survival, survival for you.

Jamie did not even remember pulling the trigger; he would never knowingly have done that to his family and his children. They had always been there for him and he loved them all very much.

Jamie's spirit remained at his house for a while, again not realizing that he was dead. I told his Auntie that we needed to cross him over and she said we could have an intimate gathering at her house. I told her that it was up to her who came. As I drove to Marilyn's house two geese flew alongside my van they seemed to be guiding me to her house. I knew this represented Kyle and Jamie. There were six ladies in total and we started by lighting a candle for Jamie. Kyle was a big presence here because this was the house he had grown up in, his parent's house. Kyle and Jamie were cousins and today the house was full of their cousins, aunties, Moms, sister in law and niece. I again was guided to play music. The first song I had to play to honour Jamie was "Blackbird with a Broken Wing" by Sarah Mclaughlan. This was Jamie, at the moment he was broken he could not fly to the next level. Everyone lit their own candle to honour Jamie; one by one everyone said something about him. Amongst the tears and laughter we then played "In the arms of an angel". I could see him going with Kyle and a few others to the light. Even though the ones in the room could not see it they sensed it. The room turned from cold to warm and they just felt him go. There was a sense of peace around. He had found comfort in the arms of the angels...

The last song I played was "Rainbow Connection" and then I gave messages to his loved ones from him. He told his Mom he would send her a rainbow. On the way home she was with her niece and they both saw a rainbow appear over Jamie's house – a validation for the two of them that he was now in a better place.

For all those in the room that day they allowed Jamie to go – the hardest task of all was for his Mom. It is hard for any parent to let their child go; it is indeed a selfless act of love. To hold on to them at this level is to suffocate them. Some people are afraid to let go in case they forget their loved ones but you never will. Years will go by and it will be just like yesterday, you remember what they look like, the touch of their skin, their smile and the sparkle of their eyes. You cannot forget them when they are right beside you. They live inside your hearts always. It is important for you to live life for them and for yourself. You must to the best of your ability enjoy your time here on earth. They can still enjoy being with us on another level, having fun with us making us laugh -when we think of them, hold your hand out feel them standing right beside you, feel them loving you and guiding you – until you meet on the other side of the rainbow.

Someday we will find the rainbow connection...

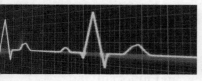

Chapter 59

Charlie

I picked up the phone to hear a gentleman say "Hello my name is David and I was led to your website. My grandson ended his life in July and I have been seeking some answers; by your website I can tell you are a genuine medium and I was wondering if I could see you soon."

I had a short conversation with David and I could tell his grandson had not crossed to the other side yet and his spirit being was in limbo. I could not give David any information at this very point in time as I was too focused on where his grandson was and did not want to say anything to David until I had crossed his grandson over. I could see that the grandson was in a very dark place he did not realize he was dead and was trying to stay close to his earthly family and could not understand why they were not communicating with him – why could they not hear him? Why could they not see him?

When I had time a day or two later I crossed David's grandson over to the other side so his being could go to a higher level. I told the grandson that he was forgiven for ending his life here on earth, he was loved and his great grandmother on his father's side came to reach out to him with love and take him to a higher level so he could be happy and at peace.

The next day a Mum came to see me with her young son who was having trouble sleeping since his parents had split up. He was sleeping in his Mums bed because he was scared to sleep on his own and at ten years old this was frowned upon by society and the beliefs of society. This ten year old was young and innocent and wanted someone to sleep with him so he would not be scared – his Mum was loving and safe for him. He was the only child at home so had no siblings to sleep with. His Mum wanted to get him to sleep in his own bed but was having great difficulty as her son could "feel" things and energies around him and did not under-stand it all. I suggested that she get a large bear for her son to sleep with so he had something to snuggle at night.

The following day I was out shopping in a store and right in the middle of the aisle was a huge brown soft bear. He was very cud-dly and adorable and I bought it for my client and her son. I knew immediately the bears name had to be Charlie. I wrote a note to my client's son and asked if he would accept Charlie to be his friend, Charlie got scared sometimes and needed to be hugged and loved. When I gave the bear to my client she was thrilled as she had to wait until payday to buy a bear for her son; when she gave the bear to her son he was so excited and loved Charlie immediately; he decided that he would sleep in his own bed with Charlie! A month later he still sleeps all night in his own bed cuddled to Charlie.

When David came to see me I explained that his grandson had been in a dark place and that I had crossed him over and so now he was able to communicate with his Grandfather clearly. I told him about the grandmother and he said that it was his Mum. I thanked David for coming and seeing me as he had given his grandson the greatest gift of all and that was "freedom". David said his grandsons name was Charlie and he just could not understand why he would do this. Charlie explained to me that when he took his life it was not him in his earthly body but another entity that had got attached to him while he was experimenting with a drug. He did not do drugs, but had tried it. He said he did not feel good enough; he was trying to please too many people – five to be exact. They all had different opinions and criticised Charlie. Charlie showed me that he was around a little brother who was about five; David confirmed this was his half-brother from his Dads second marriage. Charlie also showed me that he took on negative energy from when his parents fought at the tender age of five; Charlie had been very sensitive and had absorbed this into his energy field. Charlie wanted to protect his little brother from the same thing and even though his brother's parents did not fight they now had the stress of his suicide which brought tension into the family. David confirmed that he understood the different opinions and said that the day Charlie died he had been driving his girlfriend around and went to park somewhere and the girlfriend said "my mother could park better than you". This was the final straw for Charlie and he told her to get out of the car. She said he was looking straight ahead with tunnel vision and said again "get out of the car I have something to do". She thought he was joking but he was very serious. She got out of the car because of the force behind his voice; he was all of a sudden behaving very strange. Charlie took his life.

Now most people were very sorry they had criticised Charlie and wanting him to behave the way they had wanted; or what they thought he was capable of. Charlie was very bright but felt the pressure of his family to do "better things with his life". This is something many humans do as they do not think about other people's feelings as many have difficulties stepping into someone else's shoes and their feelings. This is not to make anyone feel bad but for you to have awareness – why are you criticising someone? Why do you want them to be a certain way? I am sure we have all criticised someone or something at some point in our life and this is for everyone to think twice about it – are you the only one criticising that person? Not everyone can take the abuse, not everyone lets it roll of their backs. Going forward it is to learn to look at yourself and your life not what others are doing whether they are your family or someone very close to you. Are you in a relationship and are you criticising and complaining about that person you are supposed to love? Maybe this is a time to take a closer look at yourself and why you are doing it. Maybe this is time for you to allow someone to do their journey their way? Acceptance is a very high quality for humans to learn as this is a "soul" lesson.

David felt such relief and immense peace after his session. I had done some emotional releasing with him so he could release the anger and guilt that came with his grandson's suicide.

After David left Charlie continued to give me messages and told me it was indeed him that had placed the bear in my path to give to my client's son. Charlie gave me the name of the bear. I was in a store that did not sell toys – it was a bedding store so very strange that there was only one bin of about four big brown bears for sale. Charlie told me he was helping young boys who were sensitive and helping them with their emotions when they were having trouble with parents/relationships around them; people arguing or being negative where they absorb that energy. Charlie was already bringing love to young children on earth as he understands now he can see more clearly; this was why he chose to die; this was his higher purpose. He had been sad while he lived here on earth but now he is free, he is very happy and at peace -now he is truly living -he is doing what he loves and that is being his true self, full of love and life. People are now ready to receive all of him; they would listen to him now and he in turn could help them.

Months later Charlie continues to help children. I believe he planted the thoughts for me to do my classes "over the rainbow with parent and child" – helping children to release emotions; for them to have more confidence in themselves, for them to see their strengths, what makes them happy and to learn easy everyday tools to help them through life. This class also teaches communication with child and parent.

I am grateful for Charlie and his higher purpose.

Chapter 60
Following the Energy

People who choose suicide follow the energy of what they know they are meant to do; sometimes a dark energy engulfs them, it is like they are in a trance and just have to follow it. They do not think about their loved ones at that moment because if they did they would not do it.

For some people they purposely take their own lives to avoid a "bad" situation, they might have people after them if they owe money for drugs, or gambling debts or any sexual exploitation which they are afraid of. Many take their own life when their lies catch up with them or when they have the awareness that they are going to be found out and are going to get caught. They cannot stand the thought of what their family will think of them, they cannot face the crime they have committed. These people's souls will come back into a different body but still have to learn the same lessons, for some these energies can come back immediately. These energies will think of their loved one at their time of their death with sorrow and sadness. For some of these suicides they do know what they are doing and plan their death. Many will leave notes behind for their loved ones. Remember all suicides are unique.

An energy that I worked with who had committed suicide was a middle aged man. He had been caught and was charged with child molestation. He himself did not want to face going to prison, so instead he thought he would take the easy way out and kill himself. He took himself into the garage, shut the door and suffocated himself with the hose. He instead had to come back to earth to learn that same lesson all over again, so in reality he would have been better off to face the jail time and learn his lessons as now it will take him longer as he has more years on earth to live. He will have to do the process of life all over again, he will be faced with the choice at the same age whether to face the court or take his life again. I certainly hope he chooses to face the court otherwise he will have to keep coming back to earth until he learns the lesson to face the punishment; taking responsibility for his actions.

When Linda's son Chris chose suicide he was in a depressive state of unawareness. Trying to numb out what he was feeling and not understanding life. He looked to drugs as a way out, only to get over his head in more ways than one. He owed money for them and got scared and took his own life. Linda tried to get him help with his depression and drug issues but at twenty one he would not go for help. What are you meant to do? Drag them kicking and screaming? When they are stronger than you they kick you. Chris was a good soul, he wanted everyone to be happy and have a good time. He was caring, compassionate and sensitive. I believe he had gifts that he did not understand and for males it can be hard to comprehend what they are feeling. They feel in society you can't be a softy you need to be a "man", so you try hard to be something or someone other than your true self. The first time I met Linda was at one of mine and Jeneen's meditation classes where we guide people to meet their loved ones in spirit. At first Linda struggled to meditate but by the end of the class she knew her son was with her. Linda followed the energy of her son. Linda said to Jeneen and me "You made me open my mind to trust and believe that we can connect with spirit. It took me many years to get over the guilt of my son Chris's death as I also suffered from depression and knew what it was like to feel suicidal. I now know that he was sick and it was his choice. As I grow spiritually I talk to others about my connections with him and give others hope. They can go to a better place where they are happy and can be around their loved ones on earth."

When doing a reading for Vicky her ex-boyfriend came through, his name was also Chris. Chris himself had committed suicide and he was dripping water on her. She explained that he had taken his life in the sea, he put crystals and tobacco in his pockets and was loaded down with "gifts". Vicky said he was a powerful energy; he actually had the power to blow light bulbs. Chris had trouble fitting in with people; they had gone their separate ways but remained friends. The night he committed suicide Vicky was with her friend and there were two DVD's of Chris' staring at them from their coffee table. Vicky sensed something was wrong and said I think we should go see him. She followed her senses and energy. When they got to his house he was not there his Mum said "he had gone to the cliffs." Vicky searched for him and called his name but there was no answer. They later found out he had taken his life in the sea. Vicky was so sad that they could not have stopped him why could she have not followed that energy sooner? She also realized that Chris had a way of mystically disappearing; he was like Merlin could wrap his cloak around him and magic would happen, poof he would disappear. Chris can still create magic from where he is. Two days after he had died Vicky was putting her baby to bed when she felt water droplets come from the ceiling onto her head. She looked up as she was sure she would see that the ceiling had a leak in it, but it was bone dry, she thought of Chris. It was him telling her that he had made it and he was ok.

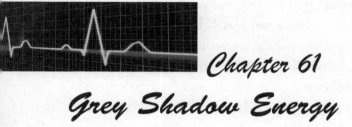

Chapter 61
Grey Shadow Energy

When doing a reading for Laura, two young male energies came through. I felt their lives had both ended abruptly but in different ways. I could see them as slender and shy – which they both were. One had died in a car accident and he wanted to thank Laura for being the beautiful person she was and he was going to give her orchids as his sign to her. 'This is to remind you of the beauty in yourself and everything around you; even in the things that seem "not nice". It is to learn and grow from these "negative" experiences'.

With that the other male stepped forward; his life had ended in suicide. I could tell that his energy had been quiet and not confident when he lived here on earth. He showed me that he had "grey shadow energy" with him and it was that energy that helped him to end his earthly life. (He told me that grey shadow energy was an energetic frequency that got attached to him, it was something that programmed him and told him how to act and what to do). Laura told me his name was Mac and they had suspected suicide with him. Mac told me that Laura had seen the grey in his energy field;

she had seen the slight grey tone to his face. Mac also said that Laura was aware that he had started to behave differently – Laura thought he had been acting "weird" and not his normal self. Laura confirmed this and I told her she had a gift for seeing the grey shadow energy and could put this to good use on this earth. Mac was on the "other side" he was not lost between the worlds because his higher purpose was to help his family come to terms with their "emotions." He helped his family bring them to the surface as their lesson was to embrace their emotions and deal with them in this life time. One thing for sure when you deal with suicide emotions of all kinds come to the surface. Mac was working with Laura as she was a truly loving light energy and her love and kindness was needed with people who did not have confidence in themselves as she would be the space to allow them to be; letting them grow in their own time. Laura was learning not to judge and to see beyond what earthly people were only willing to see. She was willing to see things in a different light; choosing to be different; to be open minded and learning about her energy; to change and go with the flow; to be willing to see this world through many different eyes. Laura had a sense inside of her; in the core of her where she could detect when she could trust someone; when people were telling the truth or trying to manipulate her. Laura was sensing the truth.

Laura confirmed that she was seeing the greys in a few people lately and she had indeed been feeling the "flips" in her stomach. Laura's grandfather came through and told her to be "quiet", to start to really listen to people and to start really looking at them and to pay attention to people's body language which you could only do if you were quiet. If you talk too much then you lose focus on what other people are doing and how they are acting. Laura was to start really trusting herself as her grandfather would be helping her with this and would always be walking beside her on her journey ahead. This all made complete sense to Laura and gave her a renewed sense of purpose. Laura had been very surprised by the spirits that showed up but gratefully received them as each one had a special piece for her on her journey on earth.

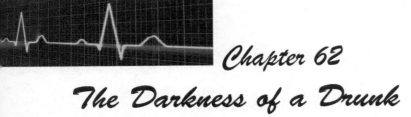

Chapter 62
The Darkness of a Drunk Driver

For a few days I felt a very cold energy around me – the feeling I get when someone has committed suicide and they have not passed over yet.

I feel cold inside to my core – someone wants me to help them but I could not tune into who they are yet, their energy is so expansive around me that I am engulfed by their energy. The cold grey ugly energy – the heaviness of it makes me sick so I have to lie down -I have to rest so it does not pull me under – so I can keep my light shining.

As I am sleeping I get a young male coming through who I have worked with before and helps me with suicides. He tells me this is a young woman who has been charged with drunk driving. He is going to take her on the passage way to recovery.

I am able to tune into her energy then and she tells me that she was very sorry to all she hurt and killed. She had got caught up in the moment of having some social drinks -she was happy – she was having a good time, until the shadows came in – these dark energies that told her to keep drinking. They came stronger and started to attack her brain cells so she could no longer think for herself; they thought for her. She could only see darkness and her only thought was she had to get home, she was ok and could make it home – they told her so. Nothing else mattered in that very moment but to get home. She needed to get into her own bed where she always felt safe. It was easy to start the car up, easy to pull away, but harder to see the road with everyone's lights coming at her – she had to concentrate so hard and she was tired – she just wanted to sleep. Her eyes fell to the floor for a moment and it was as if someone else took hold of the wheel and swerved the car – oh my god what is happening, an almighty crash and everything went black.

She recalls hearing sirens and people shouting but then everything went black again.

In the morning she was told that she was drunk while driving and had killed more than one person. "NO! How can that be, I would never intentionally kill another person, I am kind and try to help people. How could that have been me?"

She was questioned but did not have much recollection of the accident. People were looking at her differently, judging her and being mean; they had harsh tones in their voices and were rough on her.

Afterwards she was charged and was going to be tried and sent to prison. Did they not get it she said "I would never intentionally harm a living soul. Oh my god I feel horrible, what about those poor people's families left alone without them – they were children and had children – now they would grow up without a Mom or a Dad – without their child. How could I have done this, how could I be so horrible? Oh my god, please help me out of this terrible mess. Day in and day out all I can think about is what I have done.

I did this to all these beautiful people – I was once a beautiful person, but now I am an ugly, horrible soul. Yes I deserve to go to prison – I can go to jail but I am in my prison every day. I cannot think about anything else but why did I get in that car – so every moment of everyday I am in my own darkness, my own pain, my own sorrow; how can this go away?. I wake up with nightmares and screams they just won't go away. I am jittery and anxious now and don't even want to leave the house. How can I make this pain and darkness go away? I take pills to numb the pain but it does not really help – I still hate myself. I walk into the bathroom and see a razor there; maybe if I cut myself the shouting in my head will go away – just one moment of peace would be nice. I cut my wrists and feel the warmth on my arm from the blood but everywhere else feels like ice. I am so cold, so tired. Somewhere I can hear my sister shout at me, "don't do this, we love you!" But I am too tired and need to escape the darkness and the cold – it seems to be getting colder and colder – it is still dark all around me I do not know where I am.

From the darkness a young man appears I can't see him very well but I allow him to take my hand. He leads me down a passage way where I can see some glimpses of light at the end – I am so weak but he has strength and I know I can lean on him. Another man comes to meet me and takes over, he is older and wiser he looks just like Jesus but has a longer beard; he is wearing a white robe with a gold rope belt. He lights the way as the light flows all around him. I can feel the warmth – his warmth as I take his hand as he beckons me to lie down so I can rest and recover."

The young male who helped me had himself been a fun person – he had drunk many times and drove. He died in an accident but not from drink it was the day after a drunken night out with his friends where he himself had driven home drunk. He died a hero to his family and had an amazing send off. You see his family would not have been able to handle him dying as a result of drinking and driving. They would not have been able to handle the shame and slander it would have bought to them – all the criticism and hatred. It takes an incredible strong soul to endure those tests. That is why he chose on the other side to help transition those involved in drinking and driving. He even stops people on earth from getting into accidents when no lessons will be learnt from them.

The dead girl's sister wanted to say she was sorry, sorry for being mad at her but because of this accident and her drunk driving their lives became a living hell! She was sick of all the hate mail and the dog poop that kept appearing on their doorstep. She was mad that this had happened to her sister and to their whole family. "How could she have been so stupid? Why did she have to die? Why did she do this? Oh my god I would never have said those things – If I had only known how much pain you were really in. I should have taken your feelings into consideration instead of focusing every-thing on what you had done to my life."

What is the purpose in this suicide? Maybe that the hate mail stopped and there is no more poop on the door step. Maybe so that our lives can go back to what seems a little normal – if there is such a thing anymore. People have stopped glaring and seem to be sincerely sorry, the judgement is subsiding as they realize that their families were not the only ones who died that night!

Maybe just maybe all these deaths were to wake us up? To see be-yond earth, to see the different sides of every situation; to become more aware of people; to look past the human body into the being; to become aware of the lessons and souls growth; to look at differ-ent angles because life on earth is definitely not as it seems!

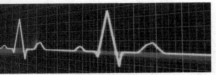

Chapter 63

Depressed

While I was in Canada I was talking to my friend Mandy on Face book and her nephew Nick who had died by suicide came through. He had messages for his family and could see the connection between myself and Mandy so she could pass the messages on to his family who were having a very hard time coping with his suicide. I felt with Nick that he had crossed over right away, I could see that he had been depressed but also because he was so sensitive he had picked up other people's emotions and just not understood all this while he lived here on earth. I could see when he was killing himself that he became engulfed in black energy, this was not him but another presence. He had done his time here and now he was a beautiful soul with messages for his family, helping them from a far. He was to teach his family spirituality and that no matter where he is he will always be guiding them. He gave specific messages to his immediate family which Mandy was able to pass on to them even while speaking to me. Mandy would text them to get confirmation. I had never met Nick or even knew anything about his immediate family only his Auntie Mandy. Nick wanted them to know he was not alone he had a grandfather call Geoffrey with him, his grandfather had met him. He showed me himself working on a green car; his Auntie confirmed he was a mechanic. I could see him around his step Dad and told him his sign was a pigeon and a dove (my logic said no way is that going to happen as I was not aware that they had pigeons and doves where his family lived but again I have to trust how it comes to me) His step-dad confirmed that day there was indeed a pigeon and a dove hanging around his garage where he was working. He also said that while outside, feathers fell from above him and he looked up but there were no birds around anywhere. He had messages for his Mum and sister also. How could I give these messages to them from Canada and Face book? Well all you do is tune into the energy so you can do this from any space. We are all energy; people living on earth are just a lower energy than people in spirit. After loved ones die we can look for signs that they are still around, we can feel them, hear them, see them. We get messages in many different ways. Nicks sign was yellow rubber ducks; he shows me them whenever he is working with me. The day before I was due to do a message evening in England he came through. I kept seeing yellow rubber ducks everywhere so I knew he was going to be there helping me. As it turned out someone in the audience needed to connect to a male who had committed suicide. This suicide had been different and had been drug induced, I felt this male was very "spacey" and with the assistance from Nick I helped to bring awareness to him that he was dead and we could transform him from "being in limbo" to crossing over.

Now every once in a while even I like to try and control things and again when Nick showed me he was going to be at another show I did not want him to come through. Unknown to me however his sister was there and he wanted to say hello, as well as help with other suicides. It was amazing because a lady walked into the room wearing a sweater with three yellow rubber ducks on. That evening there were three different suicides that came through. So now I trust when Nick wants to show up I just let him. I was amazed as I thought now who wears a sweater with yellow rubber ducks on it? So you never know where you will find the signs. Before another show I opened up the newspaper and there was a full page of yellow rubber ducks saying "everyone is a winner!" I carry that piece of paper with me to remind me that yes indeed I am a winner! You are a winner!

To me the rubber ducks remind you to have fun and be childlike. They are a happy colour of bright yellow. Nick after all was a fun person. When Nick is around his family, he plays tricks on them. He moves things and makes noises. At first it was scary for his family but now they know it is Nick and they talk to him and see it differently.

For a week I was seeing yellow rubber ducks everywhere. I went to a restaurant and on the back of the toilet seat was two yellow rubber ducks, I saw them on TV, on different channels and advertisements. I saw them on a bathroom shower curtain, a little girl coloured me a picture of a yellow rubber duck. I saw one on a plate, on a pair of socks, in stores; it is like they were following me. I had great awareness that I would hear of a suicide soon. This particular time I heard that Robin Williams committed suicide and knew that Nick was around him helping to make his transition a smooth one.

If I am working with someone who is entwined with suicide Nick is always there to help with that spirit and he helps to pull them through to the other side. I am grateful for all of Nick's help he is indeed a very special spirit who sacrificed his soul for the greater good of all.

It is great being with them but we do have to remember we are here to be on earth and to learn, there are so many people down here to be taught, to love with and to enjoy and that is where we have to put our attention for at least half of the time or more.

I am that someone who finds it easier to lose myself and be "up there" but I know I have to keep bringing myself back to earth to learn the things I committed myself to learn and remember before I was born. I also appreciate me going "up there" so I can see things on a higher level. It is still beneficial for me so I can help people to have a different perspective on life here. Balance is the key.

Rest in peace dear loved ones, we thank you for all the great times, for the memories we have made, it was a blessing to have known you, thank you for touching our lives in an amazing way. We will love you and miss you always. We are grateful for your guidance and love now on a higher level. Thank you for watching over us all.

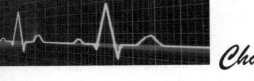

Chapter 63
I Am Not Afraid to Die

Margaret was a seamstress and I met her by a coincidence as many would think, but there are no coincidences. Margaret was meant to have an impact on my life. Margaret had sown for the queen in her earlier years and loved it. This was a part of her life. My friend was getting married and we had to have our dresses altered, this was the beginning of our friendship with Margaret. Margaret would tell me about her life. She had been married and abused and her husband manipulated her children so they would have nothing to do with her. Margaret moved away and came to Cornwall. She had a grand-daughter who she was close to and also great grandchildren who she spent many hours with.

One evening while I was visiting Margaret, she said "Wendy I have something to tell you. I have lung cancer so I will be dying. It is my own fault as I used to smoke like a trouper. I watched my friend die of cancer last year. The final year of her life was hell. She went through so much treatment and then when there was nothing more they could do, she died three weeks later. The last three weeks of her life was hell, she would pull at her clothes and get hostile. I told the nurse, you would not treat a dog that way, why do humans have to suffer like that? I have decided to die the natural way. I have discussed this with my grand-daughter and she said I could go and live with her but I don't want that I don't want my great grandchildren to remember me sick. I want them to remember me laughing and playing with them. When I get so sick that I cannot look after myself I told her I will go into a hospice. I have coughing fits where I bring up lots of phlegm so maybe one day I will choke on it and I will go that way. If the pain gets that bad I might even want to take my own life. If I do that it would be my choice alone and up to me to find the way. I am not afraid to die. I have lived my life here and the way earth is now I don't know if I want to see how any of it evolves any more. There is such chaos in this world I am ready to leave and be at peace. For right now I am happy. No one would even know I am sick. I still run the "old ladies" around and help the neighbours close by. Yes I get out of breath but then I am sure a lot of seventy six year olds do. So yes I am choosing to die my way without the radiation, without the chemotherapy, without the year of suffering like my friend. I have everything planned, my will, my funeral; it has all been taken care of."

When I left that evening I hugged Margaret. I had great admiration for her, for her strength and for her character. Knowing that what she was choosing was the right thing for her; knowing she was not afraid to die.

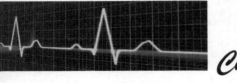

Chapter 64
A Live Funeral

I n July 2014 Andrew also known as Glamdrew was diagnosed with a rare and aggressive form of cancer, T-cell Lympho-blastic Lymphoma. Andrew's diagnosis was terminal – he was going to die! At first Andrew was shocked but after the shock wore off he decided he would embrace this. He would become a part of the twenty seven year club – (there were a few famous people who had died at this age). This was Andrew's opportunity to truly shine and embrace who he was instead of hiding his true self. Andrew was a fun, kind, loving, gay individual who loved to dress up with glitter and drink champagne! He loved being in Toronto away from his little home village of Clandeboye where he could be his true flamboyant self. Andrew treated everyone he met with love, laugh-ter and respect treating people the same no matter what gender, race, religion or sexual orientation. Andrew had a flare for the arts and theatre and loved every moment of this.

As Andrew became weaker in his body he returned to his home-town of Clandeboye, Manitoba where he was embraced by friends and family with kindness and love. I visited with Andrew and his parents one sunny day at his home – we enjoyed the afternoon out in the garden. Andrew was telling me about his journey, his illness, his hopes and dreams. He told me he wanted to put on a production – his live funeral where he wanted people to tell him their deepest darkest secrets and he would have a tattoo placed on a part of his body to honour them and symbolize their secret; he could literally take it to the grave. Andrew wanted to release these people from the burdens they carried. Andrew wanted to make a difference. He was hoping his body would hold out for his dream to come true. He loved helping people feel better about themselves. Andrew talked freely about death and I asked him if he would come and visit me after his death and bring me knowledge to help people here on earth. I said goodbye in this reality to Andrew and I whispered "see you in my dreams, love you Andrew". That was to be the last time I saw Andrew on the earthly plain as I had to return to England for a few months.

Andrew lived his dream out and indeed had a live funeral for himself. He did his production show called "Taking it to the Grave" in Winnipeg, Manitoba. In Andrews words "part of our show is designing my funeral the way I would want it as a queer person who wants it to be fabulous and wonderful". There was a manicure bar, cosy seating, a lot of glitter with "Glamdrew" laying on a chaise lounge. Andrew took private confessions from people at the show and got a tattoo symbolizing their secret which he literally took to his grave with him.

Andrew recorded a video before his death stating "I knew I was gay but chose not to believe it – what do I have to apologize for and who do I have to apologize to? We control ourselves with fear and anxiety or depression and we allow regret and fear to kind of dictate how we behave in the present. Every day I wake up and I'm happy in waking up and where ever I go, whoever I'm with, I'm with them. I'm dying but I'm going to celebrate that. Fear to me is just a challenge now. It's like what is so fearful about whatever death is such an ultimate for people and like, as soon as I cut out the fear of that, it was like a weight off the shoulders – discovering new things; more things about myself… it's like really powerful. Everything has been constructed by fear… It's not hard to deconstruct it. Live a glamorous life and drink champagne".

Andrew also said "I just hope people develop a stronger relationship with death and realize how much of a positive gift it actually is as opposed to something that is swept under the rug and not talked about openly – It's been a lot of convincing people that I'm ok with this and I'm actually happy with what's happening and I'm embracing it full-heartedly as I'm facing this as my body is slowly going away".

Just three days after Andrews live funeral his journey on the earthly realm ended.

Andrew has visited me three times in my dreams since his death with valued information. His signs are always to do with champagne and glitter. Andrew's soul continues to live on – he is on a high level on the other side as he continues to bring Joy to all he embraces with his loving light energy.

The day I finished typing this story for my book I had a one to one client for energy releasing. When she came into the room I could see a dark energy with her right on her head. I said, "your energy is very suppressed today as you have a male energy called David with you –he has so much pressure on his head and is trying to get your attention." Sue confirmed David had passed of a brain aneurysm; she had been waiting for him to come through for ten years. I could see all this sadness with him and told her that he was on the first level on the other side. He had finally stopped crying and looked down and saw her light; she had to help him go to the higher levels. David was a very close friend of Sue's. She said "he was in his early forties when he passed away; he had only come out a few years before with the fact he was gay. David had never learnt to be his true self here on earth." With that Sue had a healing angel come through with her that put light energy inside of her so she could help David to go to a higher level. At this moment Andrew also appeared and took David's hand and helped him to go to a higher level; he took him to the level where Jesus was. The level of unconditional love; Andrew understood David completely; David had not learnt to love himself unconditionally. Andrew had only learnt it when he found out he was dying. Andrew showed David how to forgive and love himself. I knew I had to read this chapter to Sue and she said "I could see David and Andrew getting on so well; David loved to dance and would love the flamboyant energy of Andrew." Remember there are no coincidences; I was going to take two days off to finish my book. When Sue phoned the day before to ask for the energy releasing I felt very strong it was important and I needed to help her – this was all orchestrated by spirit; thank you Andrew for helping take David to a higher level on the other side.

Andrew leaves a legacy behind where people have raised funds to go towards the Andrew Henderson memorial scholarship for a graduating student from Lord Selkirk Regional Comprehensive School in Selkirk, Manitoba to someone like Andrew who is passionate about art, history and creativity.

Andrew's greatest hope was that his journey would inspire people to accept illness and death as an opportunity to make life richer. The message on his tombstone reads "Embrace your true self-worth with boldness and without hesitation. Share yourself, your burdens and your joys with others. Celebrate love life and all its wonderful, messy, amazing moments".

Chapter 65
Honouring Spirit

Even though it hurts like hell when you lose a loved one so close, we must honour their spirit and their choice as they continue with their purpose.

I had met a girl at one of my message events and her Mom came through with her telling her not to be afraid to have a baby as she would not have the same destiny as her (she had lost her Mom at an early age and did not want the same fate for her child); the Mom thanked her daughter for honouring her and living for her. Afterward the daughter confirmed all was true as she had discovered a bucket list her Mom had written on a piece of hospital paper; the daughter decided when she was old enough she would live out her Moms bucket list and leave some of her ashes where ever she went. Her brother on the other hand chose to morn his Mom and takes the anniversary of her death off from work every year. There is not a right or wrong way it is how you can cope with the death of a love one and you must do it your way. I however do know that the Mom was so pleased with her daughter knowing that she would honour her in such a way.

Even though we can miss our loved ones every day Christmas seems to be the hardest time of year. There are many things you can do to honour your loved ones you can light a candle, you can set a place for them at the table. You can talk about your favourite things about them or your funniest memory. They will be right there with you. Everyone has different signs so if for example your sign is a robin from them you could receive a Christmas card with a robin on it or a gift bag or even a present with a robin in it. When I do the Christmas with Heaven event spirit guides me to buy presents for everyone who attends so they will have a present to unwrap with a unique message attached. It is amazing how the gift and message makes sense to each person; a sign of how amazing the spirits really are and how they work.

At one of these events as we were lighting candles to honour spirit someone's Dad came through for them. He said his sign was a horse. I told her he liked to bet on horses (which she confirmed) I told her that to honour her Dad she needed to place a bet on a horse once a year. He would even guide her to the name of the horse she needed to bet on. I also told her that she did not have a particularly good relationship with him and he was coming through to say sorry (she also confirmed that). I told her she expected her Mum to come through but she knew that her Mum was already there with her and her Dad wanted her to start the healing journey. This made a lot of sense to her and she felt a big weight move from her shoulders. Her Dad did not particularly like Christmas so to do anything then was honouring her and not him. She would indeed place a bet on a horse for him!

So ask yourself how can you honour you loved ones? What did they like to do? If someone loved flowers, then buy yourself some flowers to have in your home so you think of them. Sandra buys liquorice allsorts at Christmas to honour her Dad Ivan; they were his favourites and he had them every Christmas. Brenda's sister loved animals so she donates money to the animal shelter. Many get tattoos in honour of their loved ones who have passed. Some have bought stars and named them for their loved ones. You can plant a tree in memory of your loved one or have a plaque made to go on a seat. I have sat on many a bench inside and outside that are in memory of a loved one.

Erin makes beautiful handmade memory bears and other keepsakes from those special items of clothing, keeping loved ones close. She loved doing this so much she created a business.

Micha makes memory blankets and cushions for people out of clothing from their loved ones; my personal favourite is when she embroiders loved ones hand writing on to a pillow or blanket. I myself have letters my grandmother sent to me when I moved to Canada; every so often I take them out and read them. I feel so much love from her handwriting as it was invoked with her energy.

Jennifer loves to restore old photographs of her loved ones with love and care. Jennifer now does this for other people. I have seen some of her work and it is absolutely beautiful.

Thora's family honour her with a fairy garden where anyone who loved her can bring a plant. On her birthday they have a birthday party for her with a birthday cake and send balloons to her singing happy birthday. Every Easter and Christmas they also release balloons for her.

Jamie's family takes a weekend where they go hunting one of Jamie's favourite past times. They get together and write messages on balloons and send them off hoping he will receive them in heaven.

Paul's family donates a one thousand dollar bursary every year to help graduates going on to University. Paul's family has honoured him in this way for many years since his death.

Travis's family and friends go to where he had his accident and lay a wreath for him. It is interesting as in some of the pictures they have taken you can see the outline of his spirit.

Brad's family go to the lake for this birthday on July 1ˢᵗ (a holiday in Canada to celebrate Canada Day) they set off fireworks for his birthday, playing the song by Luke Bryan "Drink a beer" which describes Brad to a tee. They also send Chinese lanterns in memory of the day they lost him.

Kyle's' family sets off fireworks on his birthday and often have a party with his friends. They have cheesecake for him because this was his favourite. Even though they know he is not at the cemetery they still want to make it nice and put battery candles there to light the way. They have also brought presents for the charity Christmas drive in his honour.

Meaghan honours her Dad Garry by placing her Dads favourite chair outside and sitting in it. It makes her feel closer to her Dad. She has a shrine for her Dad in her dining room cabinet with a picture and candles she can light.

Barb honours her son Wayne by raising his daughter Tisha for him. Barb lets her granddaughter know about her Dad and what he was like even in his younger days. Barb always felt guilty that Wayne died tragically while so young; she always wondered if she could have done more, she felt like she could have been a better Mom. Wayne was hard headed and he was going to do what he wanted to do no matter what his Mom said. Barb felt she was not a good enough mother. Wayne came through for her in a reading and said "Mom, you are the best; you loved me no matter what I did." He always felt his Mother's love; she loved him unconditionally even when she raised her voice. He understands now that it was only because she loved him. Wayne is grateful that his Mom is raising his daughter, and always comes through in readings to guide her and tells her what a great job she is doing of raising his beautiful daughter who he loves so very much. For Wayne he can be a better father to his daughter from where he is than he was on Earth. He can guide her every moment to become the beautiful person she is… he now lives through his Mother as she honours him in the best way she can, by being that total support and love for his daughter Tisha. Wayne keeps Barb on track with Tisha and makes them feel loved every day.

Kirsten's sister Katie came up with an idea of an annual walk for her; the family agreed that Kirsten should be honoured in a unique way because of her genuine love of people, especially children. Even through her hard times and personal struggles Kirsten was a bright light that shone on all of those around her; her special gift was how she believed in you no matter what faults or doubts you had. Because of these qualities Kirsten developed many friend-ships and of course a deep relationship with her family. The walk is a special time where friends and family come together to hon-our and remember Kirsten and her special qualities. Kirsten had participated herself in several walks each summer, the favourite being the Mother's day walk. It was a perfect way to bring people together and that she did! The walk was a huge success in many ways, not only was the financial goal of ten thousand dollars made to start her legacy fund; there were almost three hundred people in attendance. Her Dad, Rick put on a spectacular lunch. Kirsten would have been so proud of everyone's efforts. Kirsten herself was not afraid of hard work and LOVED to organize events. The monies are directed to the charity The Selkirk and District Foun-dation who hold the monies in a trust fund and give all the interest away each year to different people. Anyone as well as children's organizations that need funding can apply for the money in a form of a grant to go towards local children's programs like day cares, schools etc. Kirsten would have considered it the perfect day with family, friends and people she did not know but would be eager to meet, all gathered together to enjoy the day. There was such a strong presence of her excitement and loving spirit. The first time Kirsten came through in a message evening she was fun, she had me blowing bubbles! She was indeed the brightest light. She had said she was with children looking after them; she was also exploring and having a wonderful time. This was indeed an amazing honour for Kirsten and she was thankful to her wonderful family and friends.

Nicks family honour him by talking about him; his sister Jemma constantly tells her boys what a wonderful Uncle he was and tells them stories about him so they will know him and his character. They get to know him through her – and he will live on forever.

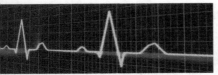

Chapter 66
Shining Brightly

It was your time to go and the angels took you away, to a place where you could rest and be at peace

Thank you for all you did on earth — I can only hope to be half the person you were when you were here

I cannot change the time I had with you but I can change my time on earth

I can make a difference, I can share a smile, I can do good things just as you did

Thank you for showing me the way, thank you for lighting the way on earth now that it is a little darker without you

Thank you for sharing yourself in heaven and with everyone here on earth

May your light keep shining brightly, may you shine on me so I can shine on others

— Wendy Terry

Additional Information

The first book that I ever read which helped me to understand some of the things I was going through in life was "The Other Side and Back by Sylvia Browne." This book made me feel I was not alone on my journey; when I read books it seems they are a validation for the piece I have just gone through. After writing the chapters in this book I was presented with the gifts of the following books: Your Soul's Plan – discovering the real meaning of the life you planned before you were born by Robert Schwartz and The Forgotten Promise – rejoining our cosmic family by Sherry Wilde (if you are interested in these subjects I would recommend both of these great reads). A huge Thank you to Jackie Williams for the gifts and for your continued wisdom.

Books I have been a contributing author in are: A New Day Dawns – breaking up with Abuse and The Energy of Magic (editor, Erica Glessing)

If you are having a hard time with anything or feel sad in any way I suggest reading the book "Happiness Quotations" gentle reminders of your preciousness by Erica Glessing. I have used this book myself and I go to the book and open it at a page and read the message. I really take note of it as it is always something that resonates to my soul.

In order for your soul to grow you must continue to learn; I highly recommend meditation where you can connect to your being – this is where all your information is stored from any life time and any dimension; it is where you can remember. I teach many different classes please contact me for any information. You biggest growth · will always come from within; you are the only one who can do your own work. Things happen on the outside world to help us look inside. Trust what is right for you always listening to your soul – your being; it really does know what is best for your highest good.

My hope for this book is for every person who reads it at least one chapter will connect so it helps bring more understanding to you on your life's journey.

EVERY THOUGHT, EVERY REACTION, EVERY SITUATION, EVERY ACTION, EVERY EXPERIENCE ALL GOES TOWARDS YOUR SOUL'S GROWTH – THE EVOLUTION OF YOUR BEING

MAY YOUR LIGHT SHINE A LITTLE BRIGHTER STARTING TODAY.

CONTACT INFORMATION

Wendy Terry: website: www.wendyterrypsychic.com
Email: wendy.terry444@hotmail.com
Facebook: http://facebookopenmindswithWendyTerry
or WendyTerry

Deryn Bothe: derynbothe@hotmail.ca
http://facebookderynbothe

Hayley Porteous: www.flairstudio.ca or www.hayleyporteous.com
http://facebookflairstudiosphotography
Hayleyporteous.studios@gmail.com

Erica Glessing: http://happypublishing.net

Jeneen Yungwith: accessjeneen@gmail.com
http://facebookJustShowUpwithJeneen

Erin Hill: www.etsy.com/uk/shop/TeddyBearLaneStore
teddbearlane@yahoo.co.uk
http://facebook.com/Tedbearlane

Micha Reilly: michareilly79@gmail.com

Jennifer Brayne – Elemental Photography:
jenniferbrayne@yahoo.com
http://www.facebook.com/groups/42139138790357

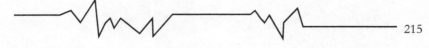

Printed in July 2019
by Rotomail Italia S.p.A., Vignate (MI) - Italy